# Disability, Work and Inclusion in Slovenia

## TOWARDS EARLY INTERVENTION FOR SICK WORKERS

This work is published under the responsibility of the Secretary-General of the OECD. The opinions expressed and arguments employed herein do not necessarily reflect the official views of the Members of the OECD.

The "Reform Of The Pension And Disability Insurance System In Slovenia" project was co-funded by the European Union via the Structural Reform Support Programme (N°IM2020/004).

This publication was produced with the financial assistance of the European Union. The views expressed herein can in no way be taken to reflect the official opinion of the European Union.

This document, as well as any data and map included herein, are without prejudice to the status of or sovereignty over any territory, to the delimitation of international frontiers and boundaries and to the name of any territory, city or area.

The statistical data for Israel are supplied by and under the responsibility of the relevant Israeli authorities. The use of such data by the OECD is without prejudice to the status of the Golan Heights, East Jerusalem and Israeli settlements in the West Bank under the terms of international law.

Note by Turkey
The information in this document with reference to "Cyprus" relates to the southern part of the Island. There is no single authority representing both Turkish and Greek Cypriot people on the Island. Turkey recognises the Turkish Republic of Northern Cyprus (TRNC). Until a lasting and equitable solution is found within the context of the United Nations, Turkey shall preserve its position concerning the "Cyprus issue".

Note by all the European Union Member States of the OECD and the European Union
The Republic of Cyprus is recognised by all members of the United Nations with the exception of Turkey. The information in this document relates to the area under the effective control of the Government of the Republic of Cyprus.

**Please cite this publication as:**
OECD (2022), *Disability, Work and Inclusion in Slovenia: Towards Early Intervention for Sick Workers*, OECD Publishing, Paris, *https://doi.org/10.1787/50e655b3-en*.

ISBN 978-92-64-91614-2 (print)
ISBN 978-92-64-77468-1 (pdf)

**Photo credits:** Cover © Claudine Granero/Personimages, and Gearings image © OECD, designed by Christophe Brilhault

Corrigenda to publications may be found on line at: *www.oecd.org/about/publishing/corrigenda.htm*.
© OECD 2022

The use of this work, whether digital or print, is governed by the Terms and Conditions to be found at *http://www.oecd.org/termsandconditions*.

# Foreword

The way that Slovenia provides support for persons with disabilities or chronic health problems is quite unique. Sickness policies, disability policies and policies for jobseekers with health barriers to employment cover similar groups and overlapping risks that are managed by different institutions. Unfortunately, this setup results in system duplications and inefficiencies and generates undesirable behavioural responses among persons with long-term sicknesses and disabilities as well as employers. It also leaves gaps in the system, leaving some people with inadequate social protection.

The disability benefit caseload is high in Slovenia; the number of long-term sickness claims is high and increasing; and employment rates among persons with disabilities are, sadly, stubbornly low. These developments have led the Slovenian Ministry of Labour, Family, Social Affairs and Equal Opportunities (MLFSAEQ) to engage in a project with the Directorate General for Structural Reform Support (DG REFORM) of the European Commission and the OECD in order to prepare a comprehensive reform of the Slovenian pension and disability insurance system.

Recommendations for pension reform were published in the series of OECD Reviews of Pension Systems, with a focus on how to encourage people to work longer and how to make the pension system financially sustainable while preserving the pensioners' living standards. Increasing the low rates of employment after age 60 will be critical for achieving all of these goals; today, only 25% of Slovenians aged 60 to 64 are in employment. Reforms of sickness and disability programmes were not covered in the pension review although lack of necessary reform to those programmes could undermine the incentives to work longer and, thus, the success of pension reform.

This new report complements the pension review and supports the Slovenian Government in three ways. First, it provides new evidence on the state of social protection for persons with disabilities in Slovenia, importantly including the issues of long-term sickness and long-term unemployment and of premature labour market exit via those programmes. Second, it reviews existing policies and measures to support the work (re)integration of persons with disabilities and long-term health issues. Third, it provides policy recommendations to reform sickness and disability insurance programmes.

The preparation of the report involved a number of steps that contributed to shaping its conclusions:

- A series of meetings with key stakeholders and institutions responsible for the management of the system of social protection for persons with disability in Slovenia; notably the MLFSAEQ and the Ministry of Health, the main implementing bodies (Health Insurance Institute, Pension and Disability Insurance Institute, Public Employment Service of Slovenia), the social partners and the main disability organisations.
- Input from the University Rehabilitation Institute (URI-Soča) reviewing their existing measures to support work reintegration of sickness insurance claimants.
- Linked administrative data, essential for the analytic results in the report, previously compiled for a project ran by researchers at the University of Primorska.
- Administrative data kindly shared by the Health Insurance Institute, the Pension and Disability Insurance Institute and, in particular, the Public Employment Service of Slovenia.

- A national virtual workshop with policy makers from the key institutions to present and discuss the analytical results of this report.
- A series of focus group meetings with the key stakeholders and institutions to receive feedback to and create a common vision for the policy recommendations.

All participants in these events, and collaborators in sharing data, are warmly thanked for their invaluable support, insights and advice.

# Acknowledgements

This work has been performed under the OECD Directorate for Employment, Labour and Social Affairs (ELS), led by Stefano Scarpetta. The report was prepared by Silvia Garcia-Mandico and Christopher Prinz from the OECD. Suzana Laporsek from the University of Primorska contributed some of the analytical elements, Metka Terzan and Valentina Brecelj from the University Rehabilitation Institue contributed to the sections on vocational rehabilitation and occupational doctors, Dana Blumin provided statistical support, and Lucy Hulett prepared the report for publication.

The OECD would like to thank several experts from the government and non-government sector for their support of the project and their comments to an earlier version of the report. This includes experts from the Ministry of Labour, Family, Social Affairs and Equal Opportunities (Mateja Ribič, Katja Rihar Bajuk, Nuša Kerč, Danijel Kovac, Janja Kaker Kavar, Liza Sitar), the Ministry of Health (Marija Magajne, Tanja Lovšin, Eva Zver, Saša Jazbec, Jana Kotnik, Katarina Ahac), the Pensions and Disability Insurance Authority (Dean Premik, Andraž Rangus, Mitja Žiher, Boris Majcen, Blaž Kavčič, Petra Oblak), the Health Insurance Institute (Špela Cerar, Ana Vodičar, Olivera Masten Cuznar, Marjan Sušelj), the National Institute of Public Health (Metka Zaletel, Ada Hočevar Grom, Tatjana Kofol Bric, Ticijana Prijon, Andreja Belščak), the Public Employment Service (Barbara Gogala, Lea Kovač, Viljem Spru) but also the social partners (Lučka Bohm, Goran Lukič, Tatjana Čerin, Staša Curk Acceto) and the disability sector (Goran Kustura, Matej Verbajs, Nataša Mauko Zimšek, Matej Žnuderl, Polona Car, Mateja Toman, Borut Sever). Finally, the OECD also thanks Marc Vothknecht from the European Commission (Directorate General for Structural Reform Support) for his ongoing support to the project.

The painting on the front cover comes from *Ateliers Personimages*, a French non-profit association promoting artistic creation for persons with disabilities (www.personimages.org).

# Table of contents

Foreword 3

Acknowledgements 5

Acronyms and abbreviations 10

Executive summary 11

**1 Assessment and recommendations for sickness and disability programmes in Slovenia** 13
    1.1. Benefit adequacy is a multifaceted issue 14
    1.2. System inequalities are considerable 16
    1.3. Intervention is coming too late 18
    1.4. Co-operation between key actors is weak 21
    1.5. The essence of a new policy setup 23
    References 24

**2 The challenges of the Slovenian sickness insurance programme** 25
    2.1. Main characteristics of the programme 26
    2.2. Assessment of sickness benefits 29
    2.3. Descriptive statistics of the programme: Take up, average benefit payments, and absence duration 32
    2.4. Sickness insurance as an insurance for long-term illness and disability 38
    References 44
    Notes 44

**3 The challenges of the Slovenian disability insurance programme** 45
    3.1. Main characteristics of the programme 46
    3.2. Assessment of disability benefits 50
    3.3. Descriptive statistics of the programme: Take up, average benefit payments, and outflows 57
    3.4. Occupational injuries and diseases 62
    3.5. Co-operation between ZPIZ and ZZZS 62
    References 64
    Notes 64

**4 The role of unemployment benefits, employment services and social assistance for jobseekers with health limitations in Slovenia** 65
    4.1. Profiling health limitations among unemployed workers 66

| 4.2. Social protection for jobseekers with disability | 72 |
| 4.3. The link between unemployment and sickness and disability | 76 |
| References | 77 |
| Notes | 77 |

# 5 Return-to-work policies in Slovenia for persons with health problems or disabilities — 78

| 5.1. Overview of the return-to-work policies in Slovenia | 79 |
| 5.2. Vocational rehabilitation under the Pension and Disability Insurance Act | 81 |
| 5.3. Fostering the return to work of unemployed persons with disability | 83 |
| 5.4. Medical and vocational rehabilitation at URI-Soča | 92 |
| 5.5. The role of employers and occupational physicians | 96 |
| References | 100 |
| Notes | 100 |

## FIGURES

| | |
|---|---|
| Figure 2.1. Sickness benefit payments in Slovenia are very generous | 28 |
| Figure 2.2. Unlike in most OECD countries, sickness benefits do not have a maximum duration in Slovenia | 29 |
| Figure 2.3. The incidence of sickness has been steadily increasing since the Global Financial Crisis | 32 |
| Figure 2.4. There are large differences in the incidence of sickness absences across regions | 33 |
| Figure 2.5. Long-term sickness spells are increasingly common | 34 |
| Figure 2.6. Women and older workers more frequently have long sickness absences | 35 |
| Figure 2.7. Reported sickness spells in Slovenia possibly underestimate the issue of long-term sickness absence due to the high frequency of repeat sickness spells | 36 |
| Figure 2.8. Sickness absences due to mental health issues are steeply increasing over time | 37 |
| Figure 2.9. Sickness payments per day have been increasing over the past years | 38 |
| Figure 2.10. Most employees remain in employment with the same employer after returning from sickness absence | 41 |
| Figure 3.1. Minimum years of contributions by age for disability insurance benefits eligibility | 47 |
| Figure 3.2. Due to pension reform, disability pension entitlements dropped by about 14% | 49 |
| Figure 3.3. Over half of the disability insurance rejections are due to incomplete medical treatment | 52 |
| Figure 3.4. The disability insurance system is complex and admits preferential treatment for workers above age 50 | 53 |
| Figure 3.5. The large majority of applicants are categorised as the lightest category of disability | 54 |
| Figure 3.6. Despite a modest increase in the rate of referral to vocational rehabilitation, the number of disability applicants engaging in it remains low | 55 |
| Figure 3.7. Slovenia has one of the highest disability benefit recipiency rates in OECD countries, but it has decreased over the past decade | 57 |
| Figure 3.8. Disability pensions are low, often falling below the Basic Minimum Income | 59 |
| Figure 3.9. Short contributory periods are a key characteristic for low disability pensions | 60 |
| Figure 4.1. There is substantial regional variation in the rate of unemployed persons with disability | 69 |
| Figure 4.2. Women and jobseekers with low educational attainment are exempt from job search due to health reasons more often | 71 |
| Figure 4.3. Few unemployed receive unemployment benefits compared to international standards | 72 |
| Figure 4.4. In Slovenia, relatively few unemployed receive unemployment benefits | 73 |
| Figure 5.1. Vocational rehabilitation is used almost exclusively by young workers | 82 |
| Figure 5.2. The effectiveness of ALMPs is lower for ZPIZ recipients than for other jobseekers | 88 |
| Figure 5.3. ALMPs are most effective when participation happens early in the unemployment spell | 90 |
| Figure 5.4. ZPIZ beneficiaries most often enter employment after having participated in ALMPs | 92 |

## TABLES

| | |
|---|---|
| Table 2.1. The reason for sickness absence only influences the generosity of the benefit | 27 |
| Table 2.2. A significant share of claims is identified as violations, with substantial regional variation | 32 |

Table 2.3. Average sickness payments increase with spell duration — 38
Table 2.4. Long-term claimants are older but otherwise similar to other sickness benefit claimants — 40
Table 2.5. Long-term sickness claimants are more likely to return to sickness leave and to retire — 42
Table 2.6. Accounting for the characteristics of claimants washes out some of the impacts of duration of sickness claims on the probability to remain employed — 43
Table 3.1. Benefit generosity depends on the years of contribution and on gender — 48
Table 3.2. The average disability benefit paid amounts to 38% of the average disability pension paid — 50
Table 3.3. Average waiting time between the application to the programme and benefit receipt — 51
Table 3.4. The acceptance rate for disability pensions is significantly higher than for disability benefits, and with lower regional variance — 56
Table 3.5. The representative disability benefit recipient is a man, entering at age 50-54 with 25-34 years of contributions, and qualifying for a category I payment through a non-occupational disease — 58
Table 3.6. The average period of disability insurance benefit receipt is long, making its low benefit payments highly inadequate — 61
Table 3.7. Outflow rates to employment are larger for claimants with better labour market options — 61
Table 4.1. Identifying health barriers to employment takes a long time at the ESS — 67
Table 4.2. High caseloads for counsellors and long waiting times at rehabilitation providers further complicate the work of the ESS — 68
Table 4.3. Partial ZPIZ recipients are most often employable with intensive support — 70
Table 4.4. Over one-third of those employable with in-depth support are exempt from job search — 72
Table 4.5. The level of social assistance benefits depends on household composition, age and the number of hours worked — 75
Table 4.6. ESS jobseekers with health limitations have employability lower than for ZPIZ recipients — 76
Table 5.1. Vocational rehabilitation most often takes the form of education or training — 82
Table 5.2. The majority of assessments classify employment rehabilitation participants as unemployable — 86
Table 5.3. About 27% of participants in employment rehabilitation transition to employment — 86
Table 5.4. The share of jobseekers still unemployed after participating in employment rehabilitation increases with the length of the unemployment spell before entry into the programme — 87
Table 5.5. ZPIZ beneficiaries are overrepresented in job-creation programmes — 88
Table 5.6. ZPIZ beneficiaries participate in ALMPs much later than the average jobseeker — 89
Table 5.7. One-quarter of partial ZPIZ beneficiaries are activated by an ESS programme — 91
Table 5.8. Almost two-thirds of Vocational Rehabilitation Centre participants have a mental, musculoskeletal or cardiovascular disease — 93
Table 5.9. One in two participants to CPR are employable, directly or with workplace adaptations — 94
Table 5.10. In three in four cases, the Disability Commission accepts the grounds for dismissal — 98

**Follow OECD Publications on:**

http://twitter.com/OECD_Pubs

http://www.facebook.com/OECDPublications

http://www.linkedin.com/groups/OECD-Publications-4645871

http://www.youtube.com/oecdilibrary

http://www.oecd.org/oecddirect/

**This book has...**
A service that delivers Excel® files from the printed page!

Look for the *StatLinks* at the bottom of the tables or graphs in this book. To download the matching Excel® spreadsheet, just type the link into your Internet browser, starting with the *https://doi.org* prefix, or click on the link from the e-book edition.

# Acronyms and abbreviations

| | |
|---|---|
| ALMPs | Active Labour Market Programmes |
| BMI | Basic Minimum Income |
| CPR | Vocational Rehabilitation Centre |
| CSW | Centres for Social Work |
| CVD | Cardiovascular Diseases |
| EFSA | Emergency social assistance |
| EQUASS | European Quality in Social Services |
| ESF | European Social Fund |
| ESS | Employment Service of Slovenia |
| EUR | Euro |
| FSA | Financial Social Assistance |
| GP | General Practitioner |
| ICD-10 | International Classification of Diseases-10 |
| ICF | International Classification of Functioning, Disability and Health |
| IT | Information Technology |
| MIRA | Resolution on the National Mental Health Programme |
| MoLFSA | Slovenian Ministry of Labour, Family, Social Affairs and Equal Opportunities |
| NIJZ | National Institute of Public Health |
| PRB | Pension basis over which the replacement rate is applied |
| PES | Public Employment Service |
| STOR | Joint body for assessment and rehabilitation |
| SURS | Statistical Office of the Republic of Slovenia |
| UI | Unemployment insurance |
| URI-Soča | University Rehabilitation Institute Republic of Slovenia |
| ZPIZ | Pension and Disability Insurance Institute of Slovenia |
| ZPIZ-2 | Pension and Disability Insurance Act |
| ZUJF | Fiscal Balance Act |
| ZUTD | Labour Market Regulation Act |
| ZZRZI | Employment Rehabilitation and Employment of Disabled Persons Act |
| ZZZS | Health Insurance Institute of Slovenia |

# Executive summary

**Sickness and disability policies in Slovenia have not really been changed for about 20 years.** A fragmented social protection system and a lack of early intervention contribute to high and rising levels of long-term sickness absence and frequent early retirement of older workers with health issues, as well as inadequate social support for many persons with disabilities.

**Slovenia has one of the largest disability benefit caseloads in OECD countries: despite a gradual decline in the past 15 years, still almost one in ten people of working age receive a disability payment.** This high share is surprising because the average payment is relatively low (not least due to considerable insurance requirements) and because disability insurance can turn away applicants with incomplete medical treatment and rehabilitation. Without the backlog for health treatments and without unlimited sickness insurance, the disability caseload would arguably be even larger.

**The adequacy of disability payments is an ongoing issue, despite recent reform.** A large share of disability pensioners receive pensions below the basic minimum income, set at EUR 400 per month in 2019. Disability benefits granted to persons with partial work capacity while they look for a job are even lower than disability pensions. Some people with disabilities are not eligible for sickness and/or disability insurance and must rely instead on social assistance.

**Frequent long-term absences are a growing issue in Slovenia: the share of sickness absences of one year or longer increased from 22% in 2014 to 31% in 2019.** This large increase may have absorbed some of the decline in disability beneficiaries over the past decades. It is directly related to features of the sickness insurance programme. There is no maximum duration for sickness benefit payments which are very high and stay high for long and even limitless periods of sickness absence.

**Claimants who receive sickness insurance for 12 months or longer are three times more likely to exit the labour force than those on sickness insurance for 6-12 months.** Long-term sickness is associated with a more frequent exit from the labour force. Long-term sickness spells lead to a depreciation of work capacity, especially as there are no activation processes or measures in place to help maintain the working capacity of sickness insurance claimants.

**Early activation is key for successful work reintegration.** The Public Employment Service of Slovenia (PES) provides employment rehabilitation aimed at preparing persons with disabilities for a new job. The effectiveness of such rehabilitation halves with each additional year of unemployment. Similarly, the effectiveness of active labour market programmes falls sharply with the duration of unemployment. However, most people only participate in active labour market programmes two years after their registration at the PES.

**Late intervention is also a major issue for the sickness and disability insurance systems.** Vocational rehabilitation provided by the Pension and Disability Insurance Institute aims at activating persons that have been in the welfare system for some time, typically for many years. This explains why only about 5% of all accepted disability claims have undergone vocational rehabilitation. Likewise, employers get involved in rehabilitation matters only when their workers claim disability insurance benefits, often after many years without any contact; at this late stage, efforts to secure employment with the same employer are ineffective.

**The current pilot of early participation in vocational rehabilitation can show how early intervention can improve labour market outcomes of persons with long-term sickness.** This pilot, co-funded by the European Social Fund, aims at engaging persons on sickness absence for about three months through early vocational rehabilitation to show the potential of early activation for sickness beneficiaries.

**Generous benefits and a lack of activation push older workers with health issues into early retirement.** In Slovenia, the systems of disability and unemployment insurance are relatively more generous for older workers. Not surprisingly, therefore, most participants in vocational rehabilitation are under age 40. Early retirement of older workers with health issues is not limited to disability insurance: sickness insurance, too, appears to act as an early retirement pathway as the retirement age increases. The upward trend in long-term sickness is the result of longer and longer absences among older workers, aged 55 to 64.

**Underpinning the facts is the need for greater co-operation between the main actors.** The fragmented social protection system needs stronger co-operation to overcome its current deficiencies:

- **Different ways of assessing long-term sickness (by sickness insurance), disability (by disability insurance) and health barriers to employment (by unemployment insurance) create inequality and inefficiency.** Long suggested plans for creating a joint assessment body promise to help harmonising the assessment process. However, change must go hand-in-hand with an end to the requirement of the completion of medical treatment and medical rehabilitation before any considerations of additional vocational interventions.

- **There is a duplication of disability recognition and vocational rehabilitation by the Pension and Disability Insurance Authority and the Public Employment Service.** A uniform view on the assessment of similar risks to drop out of the labour market and on the entitlement to vocational rehabilitation, would ensure eliminating coverage gaps and unfairness between different groups of persons with disability.

- **Lack of data and limited sharing of information across public institutions lead to a duplication of administrative work and constrain the available evidence.** This report used a unique data set with linked administrative data from various sources including employment and unemployment records, health status and sickness absence information, and disability and pension claims. Linking data across registers and institutions is possible, and key to monitoring and evaluating the labour market implications of sickness and disability programmes and services.

**Experts and policy makers in Slovenia call for a joint body for assessing sickness and disability.** The OECD proposes that this reform goes further than previously agreed in the 2016 White Paper on Pension Reform, in two ways. First, it should also involve the assessment of health barriers to employment under the responsibility of the Public Employment Service. Second, a new Joint Assessment Body should also be responsible for the assessment of the entitlement to vocational rehabilitation.

# 1 Assessment and recommendations for sickness and disability programmes in Slovenia

Slovenia has a rather unique setup to support persons with health problems or disabilities, with a number of institutional complexities and overlaps. The result is that promising support to help people stay in or return to the labour market is typically provided much too late and considerable labour force potential remains unused. In addition, there are large inequalities in the system, e.g. between those receiving generous long-term sickness benefit and those receiving disability benefit; between younger and older workers; or between those with mental health versus other health issues. The system can provide much better outcomes if different stakeholders join forces and provide adequate support early on – a change that requires clear roles and incentives for all involved actors and institutions.

## 1.1. Benefit adequacy is a multifaceted issue

The analysis in this report fully supports the ongoing discussion in Slovenia on the inadequate income support provided through the disability insurance system. Several factors contribute to the inadequacy of the disability programme:

- Disability *pensions* are very low, often below the Basic Minimum Income. The system leaves a significant share of recipients at serious risk of poverty.
- Disability *benefits* are even lower, which jeopardises the income situation and well-being of those with some residual employment capacity. These benefits may strategically be low to foster the employment of those with residual employment capacity. However, recipients of disability benefit are not under the activation regime and, thus, stay on benefits for many years.
- Because disability insurance is contributions-based, younger claimants and those with low labour market attachment are penalised. This report shows that, when eligible for disability insurance, workers with low insurance periods are overrepresented among recipients of very low pensions (under EUR 300 per month). Younger workers face an additional penalty, as they cannot claim Supplementary Assistance, a form of social assistance available to older workers with disability.
- The role of partial disability pensions and benefits in explaining benefit (in)adequacy is unclear. Many of those receiving a partial pension or benefit are not employed and thus relying on an even lower payment. Ensuring high rates of employment for recipients of partial payments is crucial.

Sickness insurance, in contrast, is very generous. This report estimates average sickness payments to amount to EUR 1 200 per month, three-fold the average disability pension. Benefits are also generous from an international perspective, particularly as replacement rates are high, and most importantly remain high, for extended absence periods.

Workers with short contributory periods face strong disincentives to transition from sickness to disability insurance. The first disincentive comes from the replacement rate applied to calculate sickness and disability benefits. Sickness benefits are much more generous in terms of their replacement rate than disability pensions (and all other benefits, for that matter), for all contributory periods. This gap is especially large for workers with shorter contributory periods, who are penalised in the disability insurance system, but not in the sickness insurance system. Added to this there is a second disincentive, by which the basis for calculating sickness benefits is more lenient towards short working histories than for disability benefits. Sickness benefits depend on earnings in the past year while disability insurance entitlements depend on the best 24 consecutive insurance years (including contributions and added periods). Especially persons with intermittent and shorter working histories are more penalised under disability insurance.

While most EU and OECD countries face similar differences in the generosity of sickness relative to disability benefits, the key factor in Slovenia is the lack of a time limit for sickness benefit receipt. Most countries view sickness insurance as a transitory work-impeding health risk, and therefore provide a high, but temporary, compensation. In Slovenia, the lacking limit to benefit duration implies that sickness insurance covers the risk of very long-term sickness, which is arguably very similar to the risk covered by disability insurance. Data show that sickness insurance increasingly pays for long-term sickness risks. This especially concerns older workers, indicating that long-term sickness is increasingly turning into an early retirement pathway.

The political discussion is oriented around the issue of disability insurance benefit adequacy, not integrating a holistic view of the social protection system. The low level of pensions has been an issue raised by the Commission of the National Council for Social Welfare, Labour, Health and the Disabled, and assessed by the MoLFSA, over spring 2020. The discussion, however, focuses on the inadequacy of disability pensions rather than on the whole disability insurance, and does not consider how financial social assistance and sickness insurance affect adequacy. Examples of unsuccessful previous reforms addressing single elements of the system, without considering the social protection system holistically, should serve as a reminder that any political discussion on adequacy must consider the social protection system as a whole. For instance, a reform like the disability reform of 2002 (ZPIZ-1 to ZPIZ-2), which reduced the benefit generosity by about 20% without touching the sickness insurance programme, aggravated the inadequacy and inequalities of the social protection for persons with disability. This is especially pertinent now as reforms are at stake once again to guarantee the sustainability of the old-age pension system.

## *Recommendations*

### 1. Streamlining disability insurance programmes

The disability insurance system is overly complex, resulting in hidden adequacy issues: for example, disability benefits (mostly used by unemployed claimants) provide inadequate benefit levels for extended periods. The system would benefit from a simpler structure, with a single disability payment calculated from the person's residual capacity to work or earn, rather than different types of benefits (e.g. temporary benefits and disability benefits). The Slovenian Government should thus consider to:

- Merge all disability payments into one payment, which decreases with residual working or earnings capacity, and remove the age component in the calculation of benefit entitlements.
- Introduce the possibility to work while receiving a disability pension, with an earnings disregard (preferably defined in terms of earnings, not hours of work) and a gradual reduction of benefits.

### 2. Eliminating age discontinuities of disability insurance payments

The disability benefit system in Slovenia is not generous but unnecessarily more lenient and more generous for older persons, and coming with a weaker labour-market orientation for this group, reminiscent of the widespread early retirement culture. This should be rectified because it creates labour market distortions and social inequalities. The Slovenian Government should consider to:

- Remove the current condition that applicants must be under age 50 (55) to be able to engage in vocational rehabilitation. People above that age may have a comparable level of work capacity but will need vocational rehabilitation even more than younger people to reinstate their employability.
- Abolish temporary benefits (right to transfer) currently only available for workers under age 55. This benefit provides an unnecessary bridge to early labour market exit.
- Abolish the age threshold for eligibility to supplementary allowance, and base it on need and residual work capacity only.

### 3. Aligning disability and old-age pension programmes

The current system is unnecessarily harsh for recipients of disability insurance payments who return to work with reduced capacity and a reduced wage, because these workers' lower wages have repercussions later in life, reducing their income during old age. The Slovenian Government should consider to:

- Automatically transfer people from disability benefits to old-age pensions upon reaching the retirement age, as is common in most OECD countries.
- Ensure that old-age pension entitlements of disability benefit claimants remain unaffected by a return to work (i.e. those returning to work with partial capacity should have the same old-age pension entitlements as those who chose not to return to work).
- Consider de-linking disability insurance from old-age pension insurance, as has been done in other countries in the course of comprehensive system reform (e.g. Sweden). De-linking disability from old-age pensions has two major advantages (and no real disadvantage). First, it facilitates the right changes in the disability insurance, including a stronger focus on reemployment and a much

needed closer link with sickness insurance. Second, it avoids spill-overs to disability rules and benefits from pension reform, especially reforms targeting an increase in the retirement age.

### 4. Capping the maximum duration of sickness benefits

The possibility of long-term or unlimited sickness leaves with a very high income-replacement rate provides unreasonable incentives to stay on sick leave for very long periods. This holds particularly for persons with high benefit entitlements and those with insufficient insurance periods to qualify for disability insurance. A maximum payment period for sickness benefits, aligned with the programmes in other OECD countries, would provide a major push for the functionality of the sickness and disability system. The Slovenian Government should thus consider to:

- Introduce a maximum payment period for sickness benefit of about one year (the majority of OECD countries have a one-year payment period), possibly differentiating between first and repeat absences e.g. with a maximum payment period of one year or 1.5 years in the past three years.
- If imposing a maximum payment duration for sickness benefits is not feasible, an alternative is to implement a degressive sickness payment schedule, by which payments would be gradually lowered over time. For example, payments could remain unchanged for one year and then be lowered in three steps to reach the level of disability benefits after two or three years of absence.
- If no maximum sickness benefit payment period is being introduced, it would be important to set a maximum sickness benefit payment level after one year of absence to eliminate outrageously high sickness payments over a long period of time.

## 1.2. System inequalities are considerable

Social protection and employment promotion for persons with disability in Slovenia is a function of a person's characteristics at the onset of a disability or health barrier:

- **Employment status**. Workers falling ill (for sickness spells of 30 days or longer) are under the responsibility of the health insurance, while unemployed workers are not covered. The former face a system of generous benefits, no contact with employers, and limited incentives to go back to work. The latter must use up their unemployment benefit entitlement, or resort to financial social assistance. They also have to navigate the possibilities provided by the Public Employment Service (ESS) and the Centres for Social Work (CSW) to have their illness recognised as a health barrier and find the adequate programme to promote their employment. Eventually, however, unemployed workers falling ill, at least in theory, potentially have options for rehabilitation and activation that their employed counterparts do not have.
- **Insurance duration**. Disability insurance is part of the pension system in Slovenia. Entitlement to benefit, therefore, requires a minimum contributory period, which excludes persons with disability with insufficient contributory periods. This group includes young persons whose disability occurred early in their career, or, more likely, adults with intermittent careers caused by a disability that went undetected for too long. The latter case is frequent among those with mental health conditions (OECD, 2015[1]), who then have to rely on the ESS and CSW for support.

This may raise benefit adequacy issues for those excluded from the social insurance system, i.e. sickness and disability insurance. Means-tested social assistance plays a key role in the social protection of persons with disability in Slovenia, as around one in three unemployed disability claimants receive financial social assistance. This share increased to 39% in 2020, potentially remaining high for the years to come. Yet, contrarily to sickness and disability insurance, social assistance provides only temporary support, for up to five months. The risks covered are also different: sickness and disability insurance provide individual-level entitlements, while social assistance is means-tested at the household level. This implies that some people with disability are not entitled to social assistance nor to disability benefits.

In terms of return-to-work policies, the direction of the discrimination caused by the fragmentation of the system is not so clear. Unemployed persons with disability fall under the responsibility of the ESS, which has a good system for recognising health barriers to employment, and a standardised vocational rehabilitation programme. In addition, jobseekers with disability may also participate in ALMPs, which this report shows to be quite a successful approach. Persons on sickness insurance, on the contrary, cannot participate in vocational rehabilitation schemes, as they must complete medical treatment first. Disability insurance claimants with residual employment capacity can participate in vocational rehabilitation, but the low take-up rate indicates that it is not particularly successful. Both unemployed and employed persons with disability, recipients of disability insurance or not, face a common issue: long waiting times for special supports, which accentuate the issue of late intervention.

Persons with mental health issues are most susceptible of falling between the cracks of the various programmes. First, current sickness and disability assessments are not inclusive of the particularities of mental health issues. The condition of completed medical treatment, necessary to transfer to disability insurance, is difficult to establish in the case of mental health conditions. Added to this is the stigma that mental health disorders still carry, which anecdotally results in employers being less willing to retain such employees. As mentioned above, another discrimination may lie in the nature of the disease: mental health barriers to employment often go undetected. For this group of people, the last resort is often the CSW and their social inclusion programmes. The success of these programmes inevitably depends on the resources of local offices and the motivation of individual caseworkers.

There are only minor differences in Slovenia between occupational and general injuries and diseases. Slovenia regulates general and occupational injuries and diseases in the same sickness and disability insurance systems, contrary to most other EU and OECD countries, where special workers' compensation schemes are in place for work accidents and occupational diseases. The uniform approach in Slovenia has two undesirable consequences. First, the costs of work accidents are largely socialised. Higher employer costs for sickness payments could promote good working conditions and prevent work-caused sickness and disability in Slovenia. Secondly, occupational diseases are rarely recognised and mental health conditions in particular never qualify as occupationally caused. Updating the outdated listing of occupational diseases could remedy the poor recognition of many work-related diseases.

## *Recommendations*

### 1. Treating sick jobseekers more like sick workers

Unemployed people falling ill face a completely different situation in Slovenia than employed people falling ill, in terms of both benefit entitlements and reemployment supports. This raises fairness issues and hinders early intervention. As much as possible, sick jobseekers should but treated just like sick workers. The Slovenian Government should thus consider to:

- Ensure early identification of health barriers to employment, e.g. by mandatory health assessment (by the joint assessment body) for all unemployed people who are ill for more than 1-2 months.
- Ensure unemployed people who are sick have access to the same treatment, medical rehabilitation and vocational rehabilitation measures as sick workers.
- Ensure ZZZS and ESS have the right responsibilities and incentives to ensure early identification of medical and vocational needs of jobseekers and resulting provision of integrated medical and vocational supports. This could e.g. be achieved by shifting half of the benefit costs for unemployed people who are sick to the ZZZS for a certain period (e.g. after the first three months of sickness and until one year of sickness, in line with the above suggested regulation for sick workers).

### 2. Targeting persons with disability that are excluded from social protection

Means-tested social assistance plays a key role in the social protection of persons with disability in Slovenia, but some people with disability are not entitled to social assistance nor to disability benefits. The Slovenian Government should thus consider to:

- Consider introducing special financial compensation for persons with disability – typically younger people, often with congenital disabilities, who never got a foothold in the labour market – who do not qualify for disability payments (because of an insufficient contribution record) and are not entitled to social assistance either (because household income does not warrant eligibility).

### 3. Addressing work injuries and occupational diseases

The costs of work injuries are largely socialised and occupational diseases rarely recognised. Such setup is rather unique across OECD countries and not conducive to good working conditions and the prevention of work injuries and occupational diseases.

- Seek ways to make employers financially accountable for work-*caused* sickness and disability, e.g. by introducing a system of differential contribution payments (usually called "experience-rating") that rewards employers with low rates of work-*caused* sickness and disability.
- Update the outdated listing of occupational diseases and consider including work-caused mental health conditions.

## 1.3. Intervention is coming too late

Slovenia has a serious problem of long-term sickness, brought about by the characteristics of the system. This report clearly shows that long-term sicknesses are becoming a major problem in Slovenia, with sickness spells of two years and longer doubling in the last five years. Long-term sickness claimants do not have very different characteristics than short-term sickness claimants, with the exception of age: they are, on average, substantially older. While age certainly correlates with poorer health outcomes, this can also be partly due to the characteristics of the system, in a context where the retirement age keeps rising. ZZZS experts share the view that, with the latest pension reform, they observe a higher incidence in long-term sickness among older workers. Data suggest that this may be statistically significant.

The duality between sickness and disability insurance fuels long-term sickness and acts as a deterrent to transitioning to disability insurance for many claimants. Differences in sickness and disability assessment add to the disincentive to shift to disability, opening substantial room for interpretation in the grounds for transitioning from sickness to disability insurance. Lacking co-ordination between the ZZZS and the ZPIZ further accentuates these dualities. The two institutions do not share sufficient information to ensure a timely transition from sickness to disability, and the decision relies too much on the responsibility of the claimant, who does not have any financial incentives to request such a transition.

Frequent long-term sickness is highly problematic, as it delays the activation of persons with health issues and disabilities. The Slovenian sickness programme considers that, because persons on sickness leave are ongoing a medical treatment, they should not be activated. As a result, during sickness absence, workers cannot participate in activation programmes or vocational rehabilitation, and employers cannot contact their employees to offer collaborative ways to return to work. Any activation for workers with health issues and disability only occurs *after* transitioning to disability insurance. Because workers stay on sickness benefits for such extended periods, often many years, it is generally too late to promote their employment successfully when they transition to disability insurance. The low take-up of vocational rehabilitation also reflects the limited interest in employment at this stage.

Evidence provided in this report shows that early activation is key, confirming what the broad literature suggests. By providing novel evidence on the exit routes from sickness insurance, this report shows that the length of sickness insurance claim correlates negatively with the probability of maintaining and finding new employment. Using ESS data, this report also shows that ALMPs are most effective on ZPIZ recipients included in the programme in the first months of their unemployment spell. The same result holds for inclusions in medical assessments: the earlier these take place, the more successful they are in helping jobseekers find employment. These results are not new – neither for ALMPs (Card, Kluve and Weber, 2010[2]), nor for vocational rehabilitation (Waddell, 2008[3]) – and confirm that Slovenian persons with disability and jobseekers with health barriers could also benefit from early intervention.

The involvement of employers also comes too late, which is in sharp contrast with the objectives of vocational rehabilitation of ZPIZ. The role of employers to promote vocational rehabilitation of their employees is very considerable in the Slovenian disability insurance system. Employers have to show the possibility of hiring back the employee on disability insurance after going through vocational rehabilitation: if they cannot do that, then there is no ground for participating in the programme. Yet, this great role only comes after many months, or more likely many years, of sickness absence and waiting for disability insurance. At this point, most employers (like their employees) are disengaged from ensuring the return to work of their employees. They can decide to not co-operate, at no cost. It is not surprising to observe substantial dismissals after entry into disability insurance. The late intervention thus turns into no intervention for most.

Programmes that activate workers immediately after falling ill, like vocational rehabilitation under URI-Soca, or the ongoing European Social Fund (ESF) funded trial with the MoLFSA, promise to harvest the benefits of early intervention. The aim of the ongoing trial is to promote early intervention, to involve and empower various stakeholders, and to demonstrate the effectiveness of earlier vocational rehabilitation for a range of clients. In this regard, it will be important to ensure trial participants have not been in the sickness loop for too long.

## *Recommendations*

### 1. Harmonising the assessment of sickness, disability and health barriers to employment

Different assessments by different institutions are inefficient and confusing for the person involved, and often an unnecessary duplication. The distinction between ESS-provided vocational rehabilitation (for a new job or occupation) and ZPIZ-provided vocational rehabilitation (for a return to work with the same employer) is meaningful but running parallel and, in the worst case, contradictory assessments is not. The Slovenian Government should thus consider to:

- Introduce a joint assessment covering three aspects: assessment of longer-term sickness with a duration of three months or more (currently under ZZZS responsibility); assessment of disability, including the various degrees foreseen by the law (currently under ZPIZ responsibility); and assessment of health barriers to employment (currently under ESS responsibility).

- Use the same functional definition of ability and disability for the three types of assessments currently operated in parallel, and include an assessment of the need for and requirement of vocational rehabilitation. The latter must include job and work-related aspects and, if applicable, address whether a job or occupation change is necessary to regain employability.

- Involve both medical and occupational experts in the assessment and ensure independence of the assessors and recognition of the assessment outcome or decision by all organisations. The involvement of interdisciplinary assessment teams will also facilitate the identification of work injuries and occupational diseases, where necessary.

- Possibly in a later step, consider options for the inclusion, under the same joint assessment body, any assessments needed for the currently developed long-term care insurance.

## 2. Promoting the early provision of vocational rehabilitation and vocational training

Early vocational intervention after about three months of absence provides much better returns, as data from the ESS on jobseekers participating in employment rehabilitation or active labour market programmes show (similar data on the effectiveness of vocational rehabilitation by the ZPIZ are lacking). The structure of the Slovenian sickness and disability system currently hinders rather than promotes the early provision of vocational support measures. The Slovenian Government should thus consider to:

- Remove the condition that medical treatment and medical rehabilitation must be completed before considering any entitlement to, and start of, vocational rehabilitation. In many cases, people will require medical and vocational rehabilitation in parallel and sequential support will delay their recovery and, thus, any return to work. Moreover, trapping people between sickness and disability – which is frequent in Slovenia now – is ineffective, if not destructive.
- Develop integrated forms of medical and vocational rehabilitation, paying particular attention to the needs of persons on sick leave due to mental health conditions.
- Assess vocational rehabilitation needs early and regularly, and make sure to reach people with sickness absences of about three months, including people with shorter but repeated absences.
- Consider vocational interventions for a new job or a new occupation early on if the return of a sick employee to the same job or the same employer is unlikely.
- Increase the capacity of the vocational rehabilitation market by increasing the number of vocational rehabilitation centres and experts to reduce waiting times and allow for a much larger number of early interventions for people of all ages, irrespective of whether they are unemployed, formally employed, or receiving a partial disability benefit.
- Strengthen the return-to-work capacity and expertise of the rehabilitation market, possibly as a special arm of rehabilitation centres, which tend to focus on medical rehabilitation mostly.

## 3. Strengthening the involvement and incentives of employers as well as workers

Employers play a key role in Slovenia when determining a person's rights to vocational rehabilitation. The approach is promising in principle but ineffective in practice, because employer involvement comes years too late and with no implications for employers choosing not to collaborate. The Slovenian Government should thus consider to:

- Allow, facilitate and stimulate early contact between employers and their employees on sick leave, to generate a better understanding of whether, when and in what way employees can come back to work, and how employers can help in their return to work. This is best done by defining a fixed schedule of regular employer-employee meetings, as done in many other OECD countries.
- Strengthen employer responsibilities and incentives for a quick and sustainable return to work, e.g. by extending the employer-paid sickness period from one month to three months and extending it even further than this for employers who are not providing the information necessary to assess their sick employee's vocational rehabilitation needs and options, and who are not co-operating in the vocational rehabilitation process.
- Strengthen workers' responsibilities for a prompt return to work, by making regular contact with the employer mandatory. Also, consider making the engagement in rehabilitation and return-to-work interventions mandatory, enforced by reductions in sick pay for employees not collaborating. Voluntary rehabilitation is unlikely to guarantee and support the needed shift in the approach.
- Provide expertise and support to employers to help them reincorporate sick workers at work, e.g. by having dedicated employer contacts in ZZZS, ZPIZ and ESS, while also controlling the process and proper involvement of employers. An independent authority, possibly under the responsibility of the joint assessment body, should be responsible for employer controls.

- Involve employers in the assessment of vocational rehabilitation needs and options at an early stage during a sickness spell (i.e. after around three months of absence), similar to the way in which this is currently done – though at a much too late stage – in the ZPIZ rehabilitation process.

### 4. Changing the role and tasks of treating as well as occupational doctors

As in many other OECD countries, Slovenian doctors providing sickness certification use a purely medical approach, with no focus on their patient's work ability and workplace demands. Slovenia also has a large number of occupational physicians, which other countries would like to have but whose potential is underutilised and unused to a surprising extent. The Slovenian Government should thus consider to:

- Provide clear scientifically-based and disease-specific guidelines to doctors assessing sickness absences, including guidelines on the standard length of absence for typical diseases.
- Modify the contents of the sickness certificate to include information on the degree of work capacity and the type of work a person can do, and provide training to doctors on work and workplace matters (this should also become part of the initial medical curriculum).
- Involve occupational physicians at an early stage in assessing people's functional capacity and identifying what work an employee can still do. This requires a fundamental change in the legislation to release occupational physicians from some of their current testing tasks (many of which are outdated) and to free time for return-to-work tasks. It also requires changes in the curriculum of occupational doctors who should be work and workplace specialists.
- Ensure involvement of occupational doctors, especially in the first three months of a sickness absence during which employers and employees are responsible for return-to-work matters.
- Increase the number of occupational physicians across the country and discuss the best way to organise the profession. They can be independent or part of the public system and they should, in any case, be as independent as possible from the employer.

## 1.4. Co-operation between key actors is weak

The fragmentation of the social protection system for persons with disability has led to a lack of co-operation across responsible institutions. At present, each institution is fully responsible for a fragment of the social protection system, as defined by legislation, without having a vision of the system as a whole. This report highlights some of the consequences of fragmentation, which include:

- There is a lack of co-ordination in the assessment processes between the ZZZS and ZPIZ, resulting in a lack of uniformity of medical assessments, duplication of administrative work and unnecessary validation processes. Rather than working on a single register that automatically collects the relevant information, both institutions need to collect data on the applicant, which in many instances is duplicated as the information requirements for both programmes are similar. This slows down the process and generates unnecessary administrative costs, and the lack of co-ordination further contributes to the high prevalence of long-term sickness absences and the late intervention with vocational rehabilitation measures.
- Lack of co-ordination between ZZZS and ZPIZ accentuates the long-term sickness problem. People with very long sickness spells rarely transition to the disability programme. Again, this is due to the generosity and lack of time limit to sickness insurance benefits, further accentuated by the lack of co-ordination between the ZZZS and the ZPIZ. The institutions do not share sufficient information to ensure a timely transition from sickness to disability insurance. The difference in the sickness and disability definitions also plays a critical role, resulting in many rejections by disability insurance due to incomplete medical treatment. In turn, people are stuck in the medical process without access to any vocational intervention.

- Lack of co-ordination between ESS and ZPIZ leads to duplication of disability recognition and rehabilitation services. Because many persons with disaiblity with insufficient contributions are excluded from ZPIZ, this leads to duplication of the work between the ZPIZ and the ESS, where both institutions spend substantial resources (and rely on the same contracted services) to recognise disability statuses. A common view on the assessment of, ultimately, similar risks, would ensure eliminating coverage gaps and unfairness. Both the ESS and the ZPIZ offer vocational rehabilitation which, albeit some small differences, have many things in common. Yet, there are two parallel sets of legislation regulating the two rehabilitation pathways, without any co-operation between the ESS and the ZPIZ. As a result, some ZPIZ recipients could, in theory, be eligible for both vocational and employment rehabilitation, for example. A holistic view on vocational rehabilitation, which would include also the ZZZS, promises to reduce duplications, increase efficiency, and promote early intervention.
- The impossibility to monitor and evaluate the impact of programmes and services offered by ZZZS and ZPIZ. The lack of co-operation across institutions is most evident in the lack of data sharing. ZZZS and ZPIZ efforts should concentrate on collecting data on the exit routes from their programmes, by setting up regular data exchange agreements with the institutions owning the data on employment and other social benefits (SURS and ZPIZ). This is key to evaluating the labour market implications of the sickness and disability programmes. Taking a step back, there is no information on ZPIZ applicants before and during the period of sick leave. Even though the ZZZS shares the dossier of the sickness beneficiary with the ZPIZ for the disability assessment, information is not shared digitally and not recorded in the ZPIZ register. This is time-consuming for both institutions, can cause errors from the manipulation of data, and prevents collecting key data. In addition, data sharing is also lacking between NIJZ and ZPIZ, including e.g. information on the duration of a sickness spell before applying to the disability programme. Such data would convey relevant information on the incentives to transition to disability insurance.

To improve the co-operation in the sickness and disability assessment, the Slovenian Government is considering the creation of a single medical expert body for the assessment. The 2010 Working Group, formed by ZZZS and ZPIZ experts, first presented the idea of a new body, the New Medical Expert Organisation. The 2016 White Paper on Pensions reiterated the idea largely unchanged. The goal of streamlining the assessment of both institutions is to increase professionalism, unify criteria, and ensure the independence of the assessors. A single body would also enable modernising the IT systems for recording data of applicants to both programmes, shortening waiting times after their application.

*Recommendations*

### 1. Creating a new joint body for assessment and rehabilitation (STOR)

Experts and policy makers in Slovenia have long agreed on the need for a more streamlined health assessment used and accepted by both sickness and disability insurance, which has led to a call for a joint assessment body. Such a reform, however, should go further than previously agreed in the 2016 White Paper on Pension Reform, in two ways. First, it should also involve the assessment of health barriers to employment under the responsibility of the ESS (the so-called ZZRZI process). Second, a new joint body should not only be responsible for all disability and health assessments but also include the assessment for entitlement to vocational rehabilitation. The Slovenian Government should thus consider to:

- The introduction of such a new body will require careful considerations on the setup and sharing of costs, responsibilities and decision power between the main involved stakeholders. As it would produce results for three authorities, the ZZZS, the ZPIZ and the ESS, it should be under the joint responsibility of all three institutions responsible for implementing policies. While funded in fair shares by those three authorities, it should operate with a sufficient degree of autonomy to ensure independent assessment decisions are accepted by all actors.

- A necessary piloting phase should test the approach and clarify the role of each of the involved authorities. There is also a need for considerations on how to transition from the current fragmented system to a system with a more unified approach to assessment and rehabilitation.

2. **Improving the evidence base by sharing data and evaluating interventions**

Currently, the evidence base on the effectiveness of vocational rehabilitation and other labour market interventions is very limited because the three main stakeholders, the ESS, the ZZZS and the ZPIZ, are still working in isolation to a considerable degree. Evaluating the impact of vocational interventions and measuring post-intervention employment outcomes is critical for good, evidence-based policy making. The Slovenian Government should thus consider to:

- Administrative registers owned by different institutions collect most outcomes needed to evaluate the impact of interventions. Improving the evidence base, however, requires data-sharing agreements between ESS, ZZZS and ZPIZ, and linking data across various registers.

## 1.5. The essence of a new policy setup

A new policy setup should focus on early intervention and distinguish more clearly between helping people back into their previous jobs and helping them return to the labour market, and clearly associate to these tasks the work of different stakeholders in different moments. Incentives for each stakeholder should align accordingly to ensure employment transitions and prevent labour market exits.

A new sickness and disability system could, broadly speaking, look as follows. In an initial sickness period of about three months, sick workers receive treatment and medical rehabilitation as necessary while any return-to-work considerations (and, maybe, all benefit payments) are in the hands of the employer and the employee. After three months of sickness, a concerted effort starts to help workers return to their previous job while treatment and medical rehabilitation continue as necessary. In this period, vocational rehabilitation with a focus on the previous job and in close collaboration with the employer is critical and dismissal is not possible. Benefits are under the responsibility of the Health Insurance Authority (ZZZS) while vocational rehabilitation is in the hands of the Pensions and Disability Insurance Authority (ZPIZ). After about one year, return-to-work efforts expand to the entire labour market and the contract with the previous employer can be ended. Accordingly, responsibility for vocational rehabilitation shifts to the ESS and, as sickness benefits end, as proposed, responsibility for benefit payments shifts to the ZPIZ and the ESS (as well as the Centres of Social Welfare). Unemployed people who are sick are treated much like employees who are sick. As they are sick, ZZZS gets involved in medical rehabilitation and maybe also benefit payment. Vocational rehabilitation remains in the hands of the ESS, as these people do not have a job, or employer, but can involve the ZPIZ if appropriate.

## References

Card, D., J. Kluve and A. Weber (2010), "Active Labour Market Policy Evaluations: A Meta-Analysis", *The Economic Journal*, Vol. 120/548, pp. F452-F477, http://dx.doi.org/10.1111/j.1468-0297.2010.02387.x. [2]

OECD (2015), *Fit Mind, Fit Job: From Evidence to Practice in Mental Health and Work*, Mental Health and Work, OECD Publishing, Paris, https://dx.doi.org/10.1787/9789264228283-en. [1]

Waddell, G. (2008), *Vocational rehabilitation – what works, for whom, and when?(Report for the Vocational Rehabilitation Task Group) - University of Huddersfield Repository*, TSO, London, http://eprints.hud.ac.uk/id/eprint/5575/ (accessed on 15 March 2021). [3]

# 2 The challenges of the Slovenian sickness insurance programme

Slovenia's sickness insurance programme faces very large take-up, with a high and fast increasing share of long-term absences and a continuous increase in the share of mental health cases. Long-term absence is particularly widespread among older workers who increasingly use the sickness insurance as a pathway to retirement. These developments are explained largely by the very characteristics of the sickness insurance programme: the lack of a time limit for very generous benefits, and the lack of any return-to-work attempts and services. New analysis presented in this chapter shows that early intervention is critical and that the likelihood of a return to work false sharply with the duration of sickness absence: those absent for over a year hardly ever return to the labour market. Without significant reform, these problems will get out of hand.

As in most EU and OECD countries, workers falling ill can receive benefits from sickness insurance, following a period of 20 working days of employer-provided sick pay (30 days until end of 2021), which covers part of their earnings lost due to sickness. A particularity of the Slovenian sickness insurance system is that there is no maximum benefit payment duration, turning it into a system also insuring the risks of long-term sickness and, to an extent, disability. This section covers the main characteristics of the programme, the assessment of sickness, and discusses how the features of the programme may be causing a long-term sickness issue.

## 2.1. Main characteristics of the programme

### 2.1.1. Benefit provision, funding and organisation

In Slovenia, sickness insurance coverage is a right acquired for those insured under the compulsory health insurance scheme. As such, only persons who are employed, or self-employed, and paying contributions to the compulsory health insurance scheme are covered by public sickness insurance. The system does not allow for voluntary contributions. Unemployed workers and non-standard forms of work not declared as paid employment or self-employment are not covered by sickness insurance. The Public Finance Balancing Act (Zakon za uravnoteženje javnih finance, ZUJF), which entered into force in June 2012, abolished the right of unemployment benefit recipients who were on the sick leave for more than 30 working days to receive sickness benefits.

Sickness insurance is funded through contributions to the compulsory health insurance scheme. The Health Insurance Institute (ZZZS) is the institution responsible for collecting and allocating the public funds for the compulsory health insurance scheme, and thus responsible for determining the rights to sickness insurance and paying the benefits. Health insurance contributions are shared between employers (6.56% of the gross wage plus an additional 0.53% to cover the risks of occupational injuries and diseases) and employees (6.36% of the gross wage). Self-employed workers pay 13.45% from the insurance base determined in accordance with the regulations on pension and disability insurance.

Funding also comes from employers directly, who are responsible for financing the first 30 working days of every sickness absence spell (20 working days as of 2022), for a maximum period of 120 days per year. From the 31$^{st}$ day, the sickness benefit is covered by the ZZZS through compulsory health insurance contributions. Exceptions to this are absence spells due to occupational injuries and diseases, donations, care of a close family member (up to seven days, and 15 days for a child), doctor-mandated quarantine and workers/volunteers for a public service, whose sickness benefits are covered by the ZZZS from the first day.

While the ZZZS manages and allocates sickness insurance funds, the key regulatory role rests with the Ministry of Health, which has consequences for the capacity to reform the sickness insurance scheme. The Ministry of Health is the owner of all public hospitals and national public health institutions, and their key manager and investor (Albreht et al., 2016[1]). While the ZZZS autonomously adopts the financial plans and policies that regulate the rights and benefits of the insured, the Parliament and Ministry of Health have retained a key role in determining the scope of benefits, the financial plan and the confirmation of the elected general manager of the ZZZS (Albreht et al., 2016[1]). This role implies that any reform of the sickness insurance system and the ZZZS needs to be presented to Parliament for approval by the Ministry of Health. This structure creates a political layer to any reform of the scheme.

### 2.1.2. Coverage and generosity

In Slovenia, the sickness insurance programme covers any insured worker experiencing an illness or injury acquired at work or outside of work. There are no differences in eligibility requirements, sickness assessment procedures, or return-to-work provisions for workers with occupational and general illnesses and injuries.

The reason for sickness absence only influences the generosity of the benefit. Table 2.1 shows how the replacement rate varies depending on the cause of sickness absence. The replacement rate is applied on the base earnings, calculated as the average earnings in the year before the sickness absence. Workers with occupational illnesses and injuries benefit from a statutory replacement rate of 100%, while the statutory replacement rate for general illnesses is 90%, and that of outside work injuries is 80%. Since 2012, the Fiscal Balance Act (ZUJF) imposes a 10 percentage point cut in the statutory replacement rate for sickness absences shorter than 90 days.[1] Employers may supplement the statutory benefit through collective agreements, although this is not particularly common.

Table 2.1. The reason for sickness absence only influences the generosity of the benefit

Earnings replacement rate by reason for sickness absence

| Reason for sickness absence | Sick leave up to 90 calendar days | Sick leave of 90 calendar days or more |
| --- | --- | --- |
| Diseases | 80% | 90% |
| Injury outside work | 70% | 80% |
| Occupational diseases | 100% | 100% |
| Occupational injury | 100% | 100% |
| Injury by third-party outside work | 70% | 80% |
| Care of a family member | 80% | 80% |
| Transplant | 100% | 100% |
| Quarantine | 90% | 100% |
| Accompanying someone for care | 70% | 80% |

Source: Health Insurance Institute of Slovenia (ZZZS), https://www.zzzs.si/en/.

StatLink https://stat.link/01tra3

The Slovenian sickness insurance programme is very generous by international standards (see Figure 2.1). Some countries like Austria, Denmark, Finland and Norway offer a replacement rate of (almost) 100% for a considerable period, e.g. for several months (depending on tenure) in Austria or even a full year in Norway. In the majority of EU and OECD countries, however, sickness benefits are (significantly) less generous than in Slovenia. The sickness insurance in Slovenia is especially generous when compared to the country's generosity of disability benefits and other social insurance programmes. On average, people on sickness insurance receive over EUR 1 100 per month (gross), while the average disability pension in Slovenia is only around EUR 500 (also gross, more details in tables below).

The programme allows workers on sickness absence to receive a partial sickness benefit on top of partial earnings if they can do part-time work. Partial benefits are positively seen by ZZZS practitioners, as they present the only opportunity for sickness beneficiaries to be in contact with their employer (see more in the following subsection). Partial benefits are calculated proportionally to the hours worked, without any additional incentive to work.

**Figure 2.1. Sickness benefit payments in Slovenia are very generous**

Average earnings replacement rate for the first 12 weeks of sickness absence for selected OECD countries

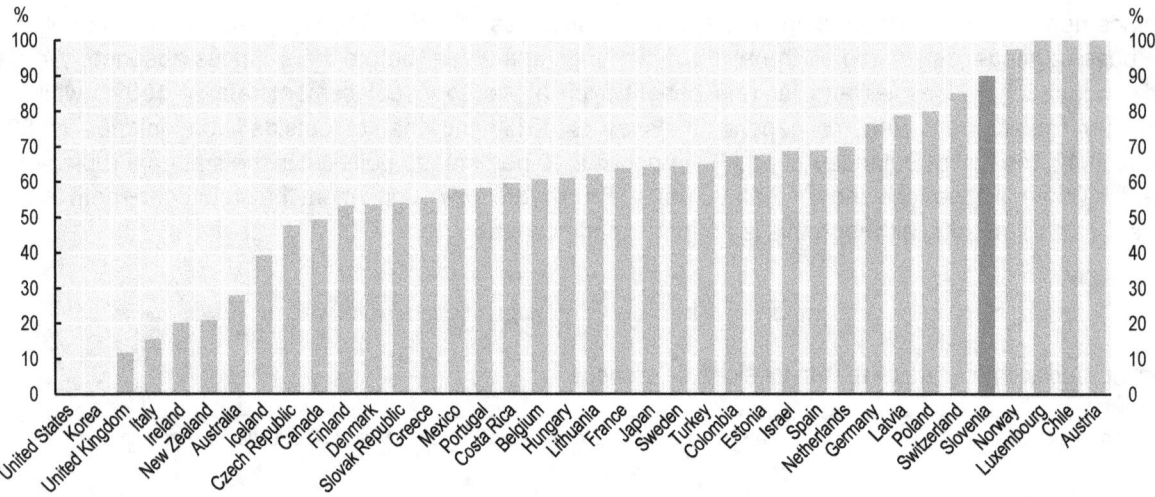

Notes: Mandatory paid sick leave replacement rates. Figures include sickness insurance benefits and employer sick pay, when applicable.
Source: European Commission's Mutual Information System on Social Protection (MISSOC), United States Social Security Administration's Social Security Throughout the World (SSTW).

StatLink https://stat.link/z36m9i

### 2.1.3. Return to active working life

Employers do not have the responsibility to facilitate and promote the reintegration of their employees during sickness absence. However, employers cannot terminate employment contracts, other than for economic reasons or for incompetence of the employee. In case of loss of employment, the effective date of contract termination cannot be before the first day of return to work of the employee, and no later than six months after the end of the notice period.

While on sickness leave, the insured cannot access vocational rehabilitation, under the rationale that the period of sickness absence should be used to treat the ailment medically. Only upon completion of the medical treatment and medical rehabilitation, people on sickness absence can request a disability assessment and be granted the right to vocational rehabilitation within the disability insurance programme. Exceptions are claimants eligible for vocational rehabilitation from URI-Soča (see Chapter 5).

Unlike in most EU and OECD countries, sickness absences do not have a maximum duration in Slovenia. The personal general practitioner (GP), the ZZZS practitioner and the medical committee are responsible for endorsing the extension of the sickness certificate, and determining the extent to which the insured person is unable to work. The extension of sickness absence, and corresponding sickness benefits, has no maximum limit. In most countries, the maximum duration of sickness benefits ranges from one to two years (see Figure 2.2). Only in Sweden, like in Slovenia, there is no maximum benefit duration.

Figure 2.2. Unlike in most OECD countries, sickness benefits do not have a maximum duration in Slovenia

Maximum duration of sickness benefits (in years)

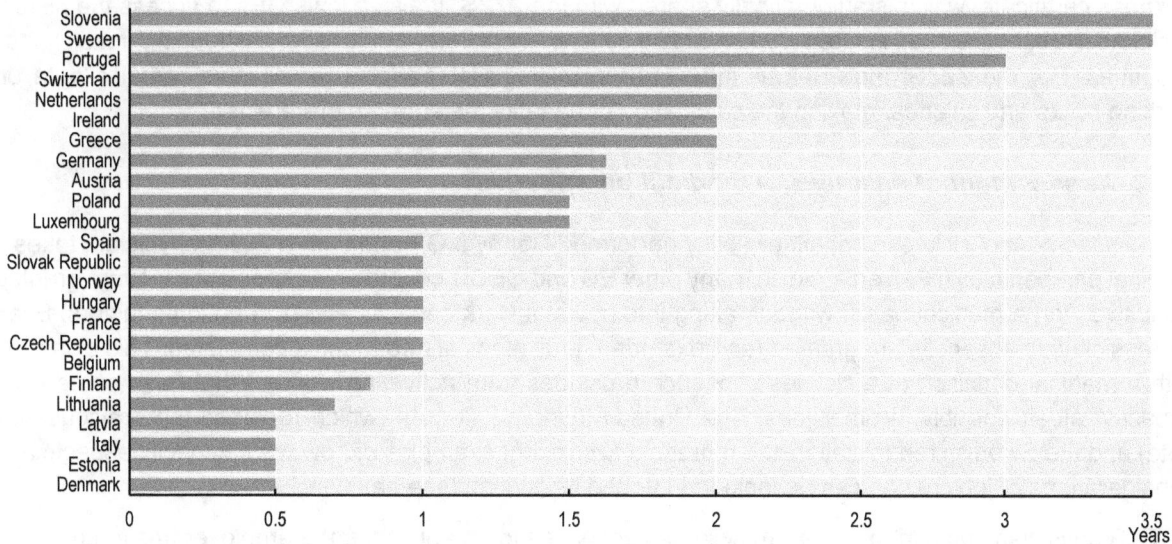

Note: For Germany and France, the maximum duration of benefits is calculated over a period of three years. For Slovenia and Sweden, there is no maximum duration of benefits.
Source: MISSOC (2020), https://www.missoc.org/.

StatLink ▬▬ https://stat.link/zl3op7

## 2.2. Assessment of sickness benefits

### 2.2.1. The process of receiving sickness benefits

Upon falling ill, insured workers need to obtain a sickness certificate approved and signed by their GP. This certificate, which includes the reason for the absence and the expected duration of the leave, is sent to the employer, who is responsible for paying sickness benefits for the first 20 working days of illness (previously 30 days). During this period, in case of doubt, employers can ask for a re-examination of the sickness status.

When the employer-paid sickness period terminates, the sickness certificate is shared with the ZZZS, whose appointed physicians evaluate the reason and duration of the sickness absence (Albreht et al., 2016[1]). If the absence is approved, the ZZZS takes over the payment of the sickness benefit. If the absence is not approved, the insured worker can appeal the decision of the ZZZS physician in front of the ZZZS health commission or the court. GPs can support insured workers in the appeal process, and so can employers.

Extensions of sickness absences have to be agreed between the insured worker and the GP, and presented to the ZZZS before approval. These extensions can be requested indefinitely, to the extent that the GP considers the medical treatment incomplete. This can be a lengthy process, and result in much delayed decisions, putting employers and insured workers in a difficult position: if the ZZZS retroactively rejects a sickness leave extension, and workers were absent from work before the decision, employers have the right to dismiss the worker despite being on sickness leave.[2]

Since February 2020, the process of receiving sickness benefits has been digitalised, which promises to reduce inefficiencies in the process. The so-called eBOL system, a system of electronic sickness certificates imbedded within the ZZZS digital platform, is the first attempt to digitalise the process of sickness benefit entitlement. For GPs, this system implies that they can digitally sign the electronic sickness certificate, which is automatically shared with the ZZZS. It also allows GPs to access the history of sickness absences of an insured worker, acting as a potential deterrent to "doctor-shopping" for sickness absences. For the ZZZS, the eBOL is imbedded in their digital platform, which also contains data on working hours and salaries, making the calculation of benefits faster and more precise.

### 2.2.2. Assessment of sickness, a medical perspective

The assessment of sickness benefit eligibility performed first by a GP and then a ZZZS physician, takes a medical perspective. In Slovenia, like in many other EU and OECD countries, sickness benefits are granted exclusively on a medical basis, without taking into account work capacity and occupational factors. Even more, sickness absences are granted (and extended) until medical treatment is completed. This close link with a medical definition of a sickness absence precludes from activating workers that have some work capacity, albeit possibly in other jobs. The United Kingdom's fit note (which replaced the previous sick note) and the Swedish rehabilitation chain present two recent examples of how work capacity aspects and considerations of job change can be included into the legislation (see below).

If ZZZS physicians prescribe long-term sickness absences to an applicant, the employer has to provide a job description. This is the only exception in which the assessment goes beyond the medical perspective to take into account some occupational factors. De facto, this barely affects assessment, to the extent that medical treatment must, nevertheless, be completed during the period of sickness absence. This is particularly problematic for chronic health conditions and mental health issues, for which treatment may never be completed.

### 2.2.3. General Practitioners, the key actors in the assessment of sickness

In the current system, GPs are the gatekeepers for sickness insurance without much supervision. For spells shorter than 30 days (now 20 days), a single GP's opinion forms the basis to grant a sickness absence to a worker. Beyond the first 30 (20) days of a spell, GPs are responsible for i) helping claimants create a dossier for the ZZZS, ii) appealing the ZZZS decisions to the health committee or court, and iii) requesting extension of the sickness absence. Anecdotal evidence suggests that appeals and extension requests to the ZZZS health commission are often a success, which shows the lack of control over GPs assessments.

Lack of training, the close link with the sick worker, and shortages of medical personnel lead to unequal treatment and the risk of overly long absence durations. First, GPs do not systematically receive training in insurance medicine, for which their assessments to grant sickness benefits may not always be adequate. There is a risk of focusing on the medical aspect at the detriment of the occupational aspect of sickness absences, resulting in overly long absence durations. Second, GPs responsible for granting the right to sickness benefits are often family doctors, closely linked to the claimant. This may also result in an excessive leniency to grant benefits, and a too low activation of sickness beneficiaries. Lastly, there are regional differences in GP shortages and capacity in Slovenia, which, compounded with economic and labour market differences across regions, results in considerable differences in sickness absence take-up across regions (see Figure 2.4).

GPs role goes beyond the assessment of sickness absence, to the application to disability benefits. Treating GPs are also responsible to ensure the transfer from sickness to disability benefits, by helping claimants collect the necessary information for evaluating the claimants' case. After one year of sickness absence, GPs are expected to present the claimants' case for assessment at the Pension and Disability Institute of Slovenia (ZPIZ).

### 2.2.4. ZZZS physicians have restricted power

There is limited guidance for ZZZS physicians' in their sickness assessments. ZZZS physicians rely on ICD-10-based guidelines that remained unchanged since 2003. Physicians are kept up-to-date by participating in lectures covering the diagnostic and treatment for several medical fields, but not on the consequences on (in)capacity to work following a sickness.

ZZZS physicians do not have the competence to qualify an injury or disease as occupational. Occupational diseases and injuries are assessed by a specialist in occupational medicine, transport and sports, or can be qualified after a ZPIZ decision. In this case, the benefit is calculated retroactively.

ZZZS physicians' role in the sickness assessment is bounded by GPs opinions, but there are some checks-and-balances mechanisms. For instance, if ZZZS physicians have doubts on the independence of a GP's opinion on a case, they invite the insured person to present his/her case at a personal hearing.

ZZZS physicians, and more generally, the ZZZS, has a limited role in ensuring the transition from sickness to disability insurance. ZZZS physicians may help in the process by providing their opinion on the case, but this is neither standardised, nor frequent. The request to apply to disability insurance must come from the employee or the GP, and while the ZZZS should be incentivising applications to disability insurance after one year on sickness leave, they have a limited role in making it happen.

### 2.2.5. Checks on sickness assessment

The ZZZS performs checks on the sickness assessment, but these represent a very low share of the claims, and are rarely binding. Data from 2019 suggest that the ZZZS performed almost 4 000 checks on sickness claims, or about 1% of all sickness absences financed by the institute (ZZZS, 2020[2]). The ZZZS sends staff to verify that claimants are abiding with GPs prescribed medical treatment. This is not done systematically, however. In addition, the right to sickness benefit cannot legally be withdrawn, for which the penalties for fraudulent sickness claims is limited to requesting a re-assessment.

The ZZZS partly relies on anonymous reports of fraudulent sickness behaviour. Through their website, anonymous users can flag fraudulent behaviour to the ZZZS, information that can be taken into consideration for further checks.

When the ZZZS assesses the validity of a claim, a relatively high share of claims are identified as violations, with considerable regional variation. On average, 6.4% of the checks the ZZZS performs represent a violation of the conditions for receiving sickness absence, as explained above, mainly due to patients not following GPs' prescriptions. Table 2.2 shows that there is substantial regional variation. Western regions, like Koper, Kranj and Nova Gorica, have a share of identified violations below 4%. Eastern regions, for instance like Maribor, have a much higher proportion of violations. These differences are not linked to a lower or higher check-up rate in Eastern regions compared to Western regions, but rather coincide with differences in economic and labour market conditions.

Table 2.2. A significant share of claims is identified as violations, with substantial regional variation

Share of ZZZS checks identified as a violation, 2019

| ZZZS region | % of cases identified as violations |
| --- | --- |
| Celje | 5.2 |
| Koper | 3.8 |
| Kranj | 4.0 |
| Krško | 6.9 |
| Ljubljana | 6.7 |
| Maribor | 10.4 |
| Murska Sobota | 6.3 |
| Nova Gorica | 2.4 |
| Novo Mesto | 4.9 |
| Ravne Na Koroškem | 7.3 |

Source: Health Insurance Institute of Slovenia ZZZS (2020), Podatki o obveznem zdravstvenem zavarovanju.

StatLink ⟶ https://stat.link/q56a3c

## 2.3. Descriptive statistics of the programme: Take up, average benefit payments, and absence duration

Sickness insurance take up has been steadily increasing since the Global Financial Crisis. Figure 2.3 plots the yearly average number of sickness spells per employee (left axis), and shows that the average spells per employee went from 0.74 in 2008 to 1.09 in 2019. Therefore, every employee in Slovenia has, on average, more than one sickness spell per year.

Figure 2.3. The incidence of sickness has been steadily increasing since the Global Financial Crisis

Yearly average number of sickness spells per employee by age group

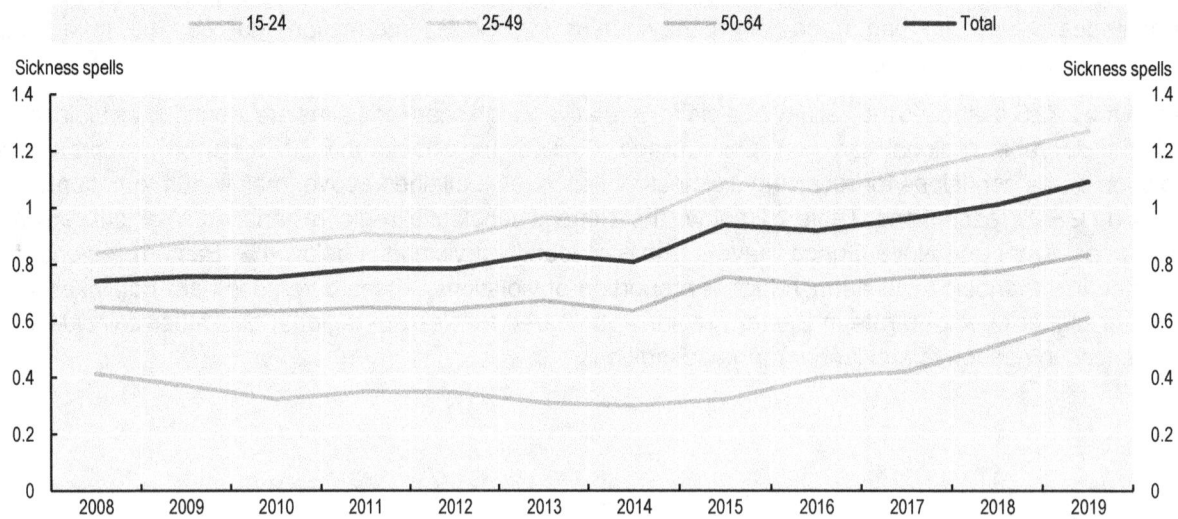

Note: Sickness spells per employee are all sickness incidences in a given year divided by the number of employed persons in that year.
Source: OECD calculations based on data from the National Institute of Public Health (NIJZ) www.nijz.si/en and Eurostat LFS employment data (accessed 3 February 2021).

StatLink ⟶ https://stat.link/iwlvgs

Incidence of sickness absences has increased for all age groups in the last five years, but particularly for younger workers. As shown in Figure 2.3, the average number of sickness spells for workers aged 15 to 24 has doubled in only five years, compared to a 30% increase overall. For the younger age bracket, while the number of employed has declined over time, the number of sickness cases has remained steady.

There are large regional differences in the incidence of sickness absences, corresponding with an ageing of the population. Sickness receipt rates vary substantially across the Slovenian territory, with some regions having an average of less than one sickness spell per employee per year, while others have an average of 1.3 to 1.7 (Figure 2.4). There is not a clear correlation behind these regional differences in sickness insurance take up and regional economic conditions, neither positively nor negatively.

Figure 2.4. There are large differences in the incidence of sickness absences across regions

Regional differences in yearly average sickness spells, 2019

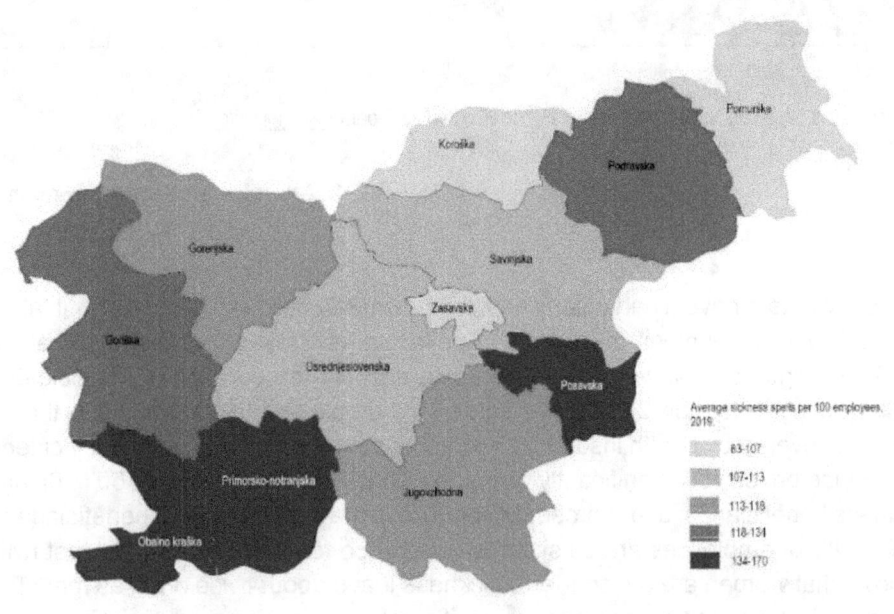

Source: OECD calculations based on data from the National Institute of Public Health (NIJZ) www.nijz.si/en and the Statistical Office of the Republic of Slovenia (SURS) www.stat.si/statweb/en.

There is a gradual shift over time in the composition of sickness spells, as long-term sickness spells become increasingly common. Figure 2.5 decomposes sickness spells of 45 days[3] or longer by duration of the spell, and shows that over time, the proportion of sickness spells of two years and more is increasing: from 6% of all ZZZS-financed sickness spells in 2014, to 14% in 2019. Sickness spells of six months or longer represent half of the spells longer than 45 days, particularly in more recent years.

## Figure 2.5. Long-term sickness spells are increasingly common

Decomposition of sickness insurance absences longer than 30 working days by duration of absence, 2014-19

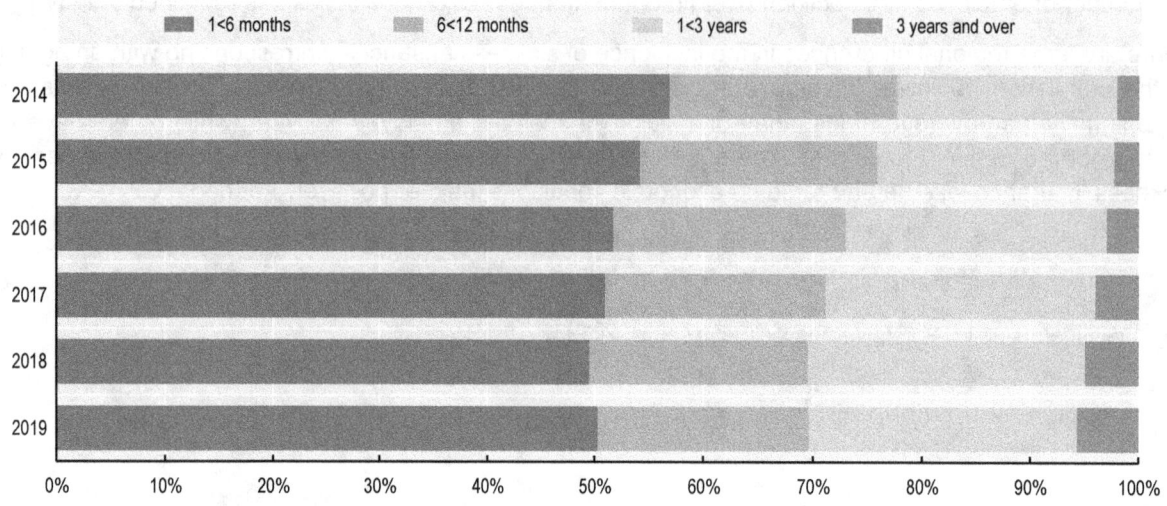

Source: OECD calculations based on National Institute of Public Health (NIJZ) data, www.nijz.si/en.

StatLink 🔗 https://stat.link/qzlr14

Women and older workers have a particularly high long-term sickness insurance benefit take up. Figure 2.3 showed that the average number of sickness spells per employee increased for all age groups in recent years. These figures, however, do not take into account the duration of the sickness spell, which, when under 30 working days (now 20 days), is paid by the employer. Figure 2.6 shows that, when focusing on sickness spells covered by health insurance and accounting for repeat spells, the incidence of sickness insurance receipt increases very significantly with age. Workers from age groups 50 to 64 have the highest shares of sickness beneficiaries, and represent over 50% of the total number of beneficiaries. Among those aged 55 to 59, 1.4% of employees are on sickness insurance for over 30 days, at least twice a year. The figure also shows that women are on long-term sickness leave about twice often as men. Experts suggest that this can be partly explained by the gender-specific pattern in the causes of sickness absence: women often take long-term sickness leave during pregnancy, in addition to having different diagnoses that require longer-term sickness leave, for example mental illnesses.

## Figure 2.6. Women and older workers more frequently have long sickness absences
Share of sickness insurance beneficiaries over employed population, by age group and gender, 2019

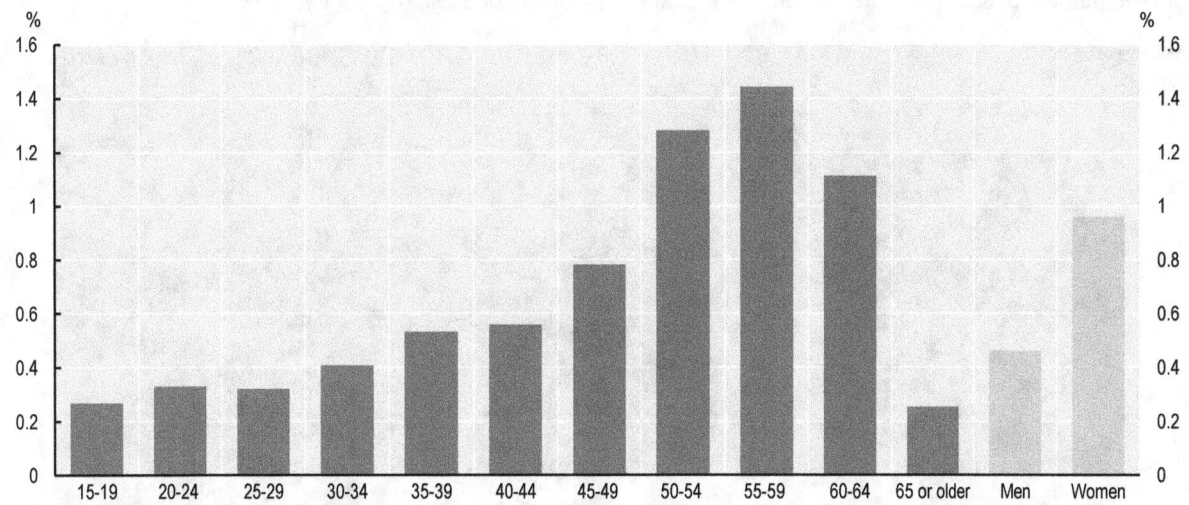

Note: Included beneficiaries are those with at least two sickness spells longer than 30 working days (e.g. covered by sickness insurance).
Source: OECD calculations based on National Institute of Public Health (NIJZ) sickness data (www.nijz.si/en) and Statistical Office of the Republic of Slovenia (SURS) employment data (www.stat.si/).

StatLink ⟶ https://stat.link/4z9jgb

Reported sickness spells possibly underestimate the issue of long-term sickness due to the dynamic nature of sickness absences. Statistics reporting sickness spells, like unemployment spells, relate to the period of continued sickness leave. Persons on sickness leave repeatedly over the year may not appear in the statistics as long-term cases, even if the cumulated absence over the year would clearly identify them as de facto long-term absentees. In the Slovenian case, where only employed persons are eligible for sickness insurance, and where the dismissal of persons on sickness leave is difficult, the issue of repeated sickness periods can be particularly important. As Figure 2.7 shows, on average Slovenian workers with longer-term absence spells (i.e. any spell of 45 days and longer) experience over two sickness spells per year, compared to 1.2 such longer spells in the Netherlands and 1.4 in Belgium. Presenting these statistics differently, in 2019 there were over 6 700 persons in Slovenia who had at least two sickness spells covered by the ZZZS within the year.

Figure 2.7. Reported sickness spells in Slovenia possibly underestimate the issue of long-term sickness absence due to the high frequency of repeat sickness spells

Average number of spells per year of persons with at least one longer spell, by country, 2019

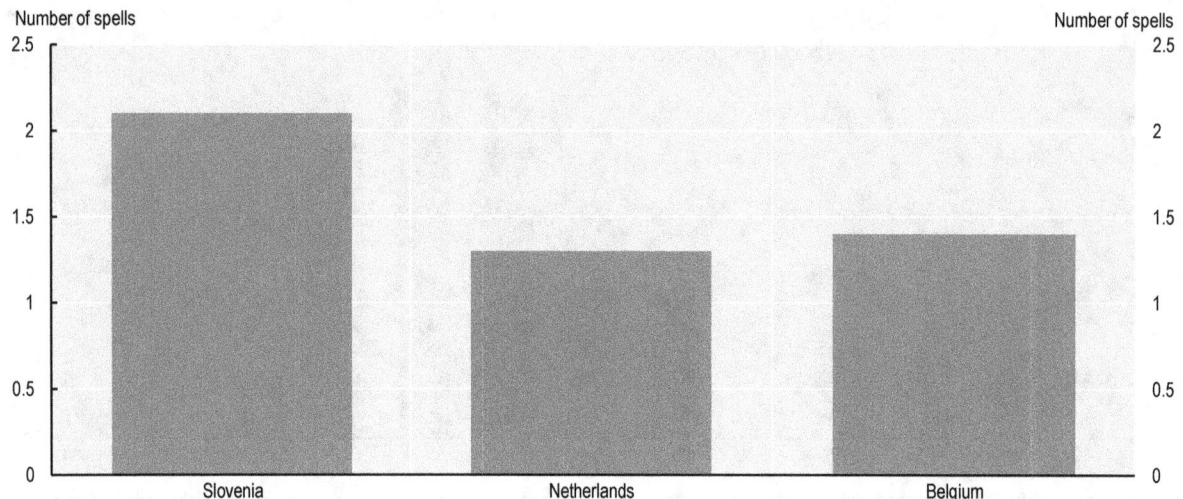

Source: Slovenia's National Institute of Public Health (NIJZ) www.nijz.si/en, Statistics Netherlands (CBS) www.cbs.nl/en-gb and SDworx www.sdworx.be/nl-be for Belgium.

StatLink ᐅ https://stat.link/ouqc7k

Sickness absences due to mental health issues are steeply increasing over time, while absences for other key causes remain constant. Figure 2.8 shows the proportion of sickness claimants for one year or longer over the total number of sickness claimants for those qualifying through mental health diseases, cardiovascular diseases (CVD), diabetes, and work injuries. The proportion of long-term claims among all sickness claims with a mental health condition has doubled since 2012, from 1.3% to 2.6% in 2017. For the other health conditions reported, these shares have remained constant.[4] Figure 2.8 illustrates the need to pay particular attention to mental health issues as a cause of sickness absence, which increasingly lead to very long sickness spells and may be affected in different ways by the rules and regulations of the sickness and disability insurance programmes. This is even more important than the data suggest because it is well known that, due to widespread stigma and discrimination, mental health conditions tend to be vastly underreported as a reason for sickness absence in all OECD countries (OECD, 2015[3]).

Figure 2.8. Sickness absences due to mental health issues are steeply increasing over time

Share of claimants ending their sickness spell in a given year with spell duration of one year or more, over all claimants ending their sickness spell in that same year, by type of illness

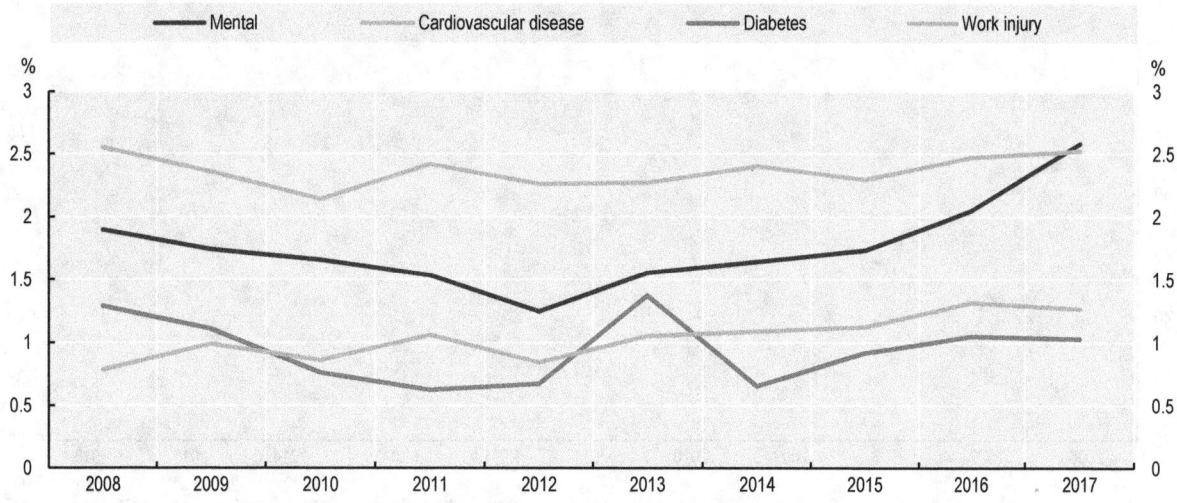

Source: OECD calculations using linked administrative data from National Institute of Public Health (NIJZ).

StatLink https://stat.link/oe7lqs

Data on average sickness payments are not readily available. Statistics on average sickness payments by the ZZZS are not regularly published and were not available for this report. Replacement rates suggest that benefits are possibly high, at least from an international point of view and when compared to other forms of social support (described in the following sections). This is, however, an imperfect measure of the (relative) generosity of the system. Another approach is to use the yearly expenditures on benefit payments for sickness absences by the ZZZS, the number of days of sickness covered by the public institute, and estimate a daily benefit payment. According to the (ZZZS, 2020[2]), in 2019 sickness benefit expenditures amounted to EUR 381 553 163, and the institute covered 6 730 227 days of absence. This results in an average gross benefit of EUR 56.7 per day, or EUR 680 per month. For comparison, the 2020 minimum wage was set at EUR 940 per month (gross), and gross average monthly earnings in 2018 were EUR 1 719 (EUROSTAT, n.d.[4]).

Sickness payments of spells funded by the insurance have been increasing over the past years. A last approach to approximate sickness payments is to use average wage in the year before sick leave and the replacement rates to calculate the (theoretical) sickness payment. Figure 2.9 reports the daily payment from using this approach, from 2006 to 2016. The figure shows a steady increase from 2006 to 2014 in the average payments made to sickness beneficiaries with spells 30 days or longer. The generosity of sickness insurance appears to have increased over time, in line with the increasing trend in average wages. Since other social supports are determined at the monthly level, it is useful to transform the daily sickness payments into monthly payments.[5] Data show that average sickness payments increase with spell duration. This is in line with a higher replacement rate for spell durations of 90 days or longer. It could also be the result of the fact that older workers, who usually have higher earnings, are over-represented among long-term sickness beneficiaries. The increase in average sick pay for longer spell duration, however, could also suggest a selection bias, as those who benefit most from sickness insurance appear to stay on the programme for a longer period.

Figure 2.9. Sickness payments per day have been increasing over the past years

Sickness benefits per day for sickness beneficiaries with spells longer than 30 working days

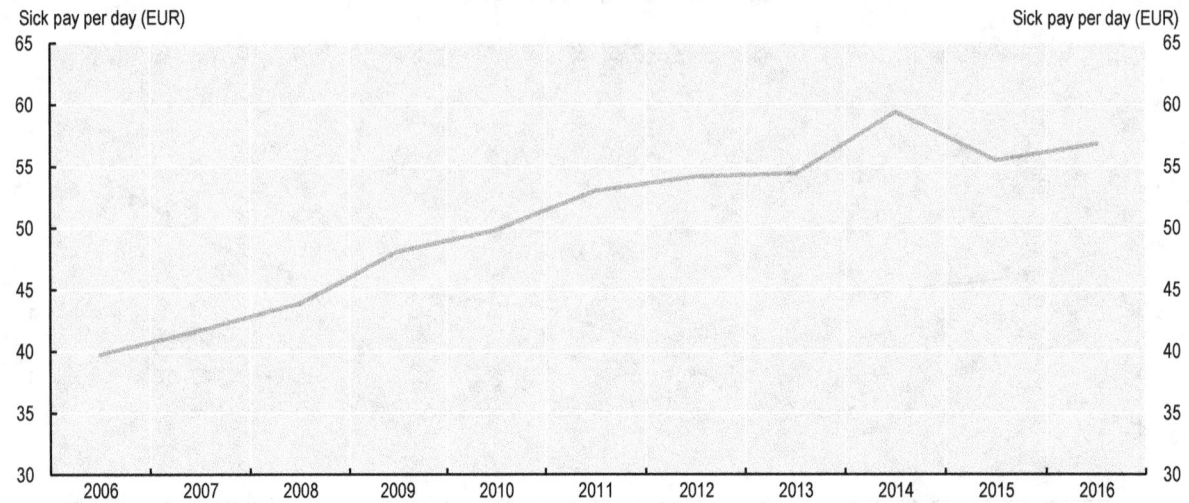

Note: Sickness pay (gross) per day calculated from pre-sickness wages for sickness beneficiaries with spells longer than 30 working days. These data include only claimants on sickness leave due to the four diagnosis available in the data: mental health, cardiovascular disease, diabetes or work injury.
Source: OECD calculations using linked administrative data from National Institute of Public Health (NIJZ).

StatLink https://stat.link/rflnut

Table 2.3. Average sickness payments increase with spell duration

Average monthly sickness payments per spell duration, 2015 and 2016, in EUR

|  | 2015 | 2016 |
| --- | --- | --- |
| <1 month | 286.21 | 283.65 |
| 1-<3 months | 722.19 | 716.36 |
| 3-<6 months | 995.99 | 997.20 |
| 6 months – <1 year | 1 113.98 | 1 103.99 |
| 1-3 years | 1 291.22 | 1 284.34 |

Note: Sickness pay (gross) calculated from pre-sickness wages for sickness beneficiaries. These data include only claimants on sickness leave due to the four diagnosis available in the data: mental health, cardiovascular disease, diabetes or work injury.
Source: OECD calculations using linked administrative data from National Institute of Public Health (NIJZ).

StatLink https://stat.link/czfaj0

## 2.4. Sickness insurance as an insurance for long-term illness and disability

As longer-term sickness absences increase, sickness benefit expenditures are expanding. Descriptive statistics of the sickness insurance programme show that longer-term sickness is increasing. There is a shift in the composition of sickness absences, with sicknesses of one year and longer and even two years and longer, increasing and occupying a larger share of all absences. This represents a massive cost for the ZZZS, which is fully responsible for covering the cash benefits to workers on sick leave beyond

30 working days of sickness. In fact, sickness benefit expenditures have increased by 55% from 2015 to 2019, and per-day benefit expenditures by 13% (ZZZS, 2020[2]; ZZZS, 2016[5]).

The assessment of sickness may be partly responsible for causing the long-term sickness trend. Assessment for sickness insurance entitlements hinges on medical files entirely, and does not take into account the work capacity of the claimants. In addition, sickness can only end upon completion of medical treatment while on sickness leave. This may lead to long-term sicknesses through two mechanisms:

- Completion of medical treatment or medical rehabilitation may be difficult to assess when it comes to sicknesses that do not have a medical treatment with a clear end (such as some mental health conditions), resulting in overly long sickness absences. Descriptive statistics of the programme suggest that this may indeed be the case, as claimants with mental health conditions have a high, and increasing, share of sicknesses longer than one year.
- The long waiting times in the health care system in Slovenia make the condition of completion of medical treatment and medical rehabilitation inherently difficult. ZZZS experts estimate that almost one-third of long-term sicknesses could be due to the lack of timely health care access. The Slovenian health care system experiences further strain currently from the COVID-19 pandemic, which threatens to further extend the duration of sickness absence.

The features of the sickness insurance system could also be partly responsible for the increase in long-term sickness. The lack of maximum duration of publicly funded sickness benefits, the generosity of the benefits (especially compared to disability benefit), and the limited checks on sickness absences could play a key role in discouraging sickness claimants from returning to work (or applying for disability benefit – see below). At the same time, the limited financial costs of sickness born by employers, and the fact that they cannot remain in contact with their employees on sickness leave, prevents them from facilitating the return to work of their employees.

Who are long-term sickness beneficiaries? Older workers, slightly lower-paid, but otherwise with similar characteristics than other claimants. Table 2.4 shows that the individual characteristics of the typical long-term sickness claimant are quite similar to those of short-term sickness claimants in terms of educational attainment, employment characteristics (type of contract, shift work, working hours), and intensity of health shock. Otherwise, short-term sickness claimants are most often women working as professionals (i.e. health, teaching, science, legal and IT professionals) while claimants with longer durations are most often men working as craft or related trade workers. Wage seems to correlate negatively with the length of sickness absence, and age positively.[6]

What are the consequences of long-term sickness spells? A context of lack of activation and employment protection. To answer what happens to employees returning from sickness leave, it is important to keep in mind two factors (discussed in some detail in later parts of this report). First, long-term sickness spells may lead to a depreciation of the working capacity, particularly accentuated by the fact that there are no processes or measures seeking to maintain the working capacity of sickness insurance claimants. Second, employers cannot easily fire employees while on sick leave. Many will thus wait for their employees to return to work before firing them without any logistical hassle. In view of these factors, it is likely that employees staying longer on sick leave will have a harder time going back to work.

Table 2.4. Long-term claimants are older but otherwise similar to other sickness benefit claimants

Modal characteristics of sickness insurance claimants by duration of sickness spell, 2015-17

| Duration | Age | Education | Employment contract | Gender | Health shock | Occupation | Reason | Shift work | Wage quintile | Work hours |
|---|---|---|---|---|---|---|---|---|---|---|
| <1 month | 25-49 years | Upper secondary | Permanent contract | Women | Moderate | Professionals | Illness | 1 shift | 3rd quintile | Full-time |
| 1<6 months | 25-49 years | Upper secondary | Permanent contract | Men | Moderate | Craft and related trades workers | Illness | 1 shift | 3rd quintile | Full-time |
| 6<12 months | 25-49 years | Upper secondary | Permanent contract | Men | Moderate | Craft and related trades workers | Illness | 1 shift | 2nd quintile | Full-time |
| 1+ year | 50-64 years | Upper secondary | Permanent contract | Men | Moderate | Craft and related trades workers | Illness | 1 shift | 2nd quintile | Full-time |

Note: Moderate health shock refers to claimants registered in pharmacy records (i.e. taking medication) during the months before sick leave.
Source: OECD calculations using linked administrative data from National Institute of Public Health (NIJZ).

StatLink https://stat.link/khxace

Understanding the consequences of (long-term) sickness absences requires linking administrative records. Data on the exit routes from the programme are not readily available to the ZZZS, which limits the institution's ability to evaluating the labour market implications of sickness insurance. NIJZ data record the termination date of a sickness spell but contain no information on where to the insured person transfers. Employment data, collected by the ZZZS and managed by both the Statistical Office (SURS) and the Employment Service of Slovenia (ESS), are not linked to sickness insurance records. Neither are disability insurance data, collected through the Pension and Disability Insurance Institute (ZPIZ). There is a legal precedent for linking these three sources of data for research purposes, but again, current data protection regulations prevent this from being a regular operation. Improved data availability is the key for building the evidence needed to inform the direction of reform. This report uses administrative data from multiple registers, owned by different authorities, to study the exit routes from sickness insurance.

Most employees remain in employment with the same employer after returning from sickness absence. Figure 2.10 follows sickness insurance claimants who were absent from work for 1<6 months (Panel A), 6<12 months (Panel B) and 12 months or longer (Panel C), for up to one year after the termination of their sickness claim. Regardless of the length of absence, month zero marks the exit from sickness insurance, where all claimants are formally still in employment, which is a condition to receiving sickness insurance in the first place. At month one, i.e. one month after the termination of their sickness claim, there is a substantial drop in the probability of being in employment with the same employer. At the end of the observation period, i.e. one year after ending a sickness insurance claim, over 50% of employees have remained employed with their current employer. This is a large share for international standards, possibly because only employed workers are entitled to sickness benefits.

Persons terminating a long-term sickness insurance claim have a much lower probability of remaining in employment. Figure 2.10 shows that the largest difference in exit pathways across different claim durations arise during the first month after ending a claim. For intermediate and long-term claims (6<12 months, and 12 months or longer) the initial drop in the probability to stay with the same employer is large compared to that of claimants on sickness leave for 1<6 months. After the first month, the trends over time in the exit from employment are quite similar across all claim durations. This is consistent with employers postponing the discharge of their employees on sick leave to the moment they return to work.

**Figure 2.10. Most employees remain in employment with the same employer after returning from sickness absence**

Exit pathways from sickness insurance by claim duration, average for the years 2013-17

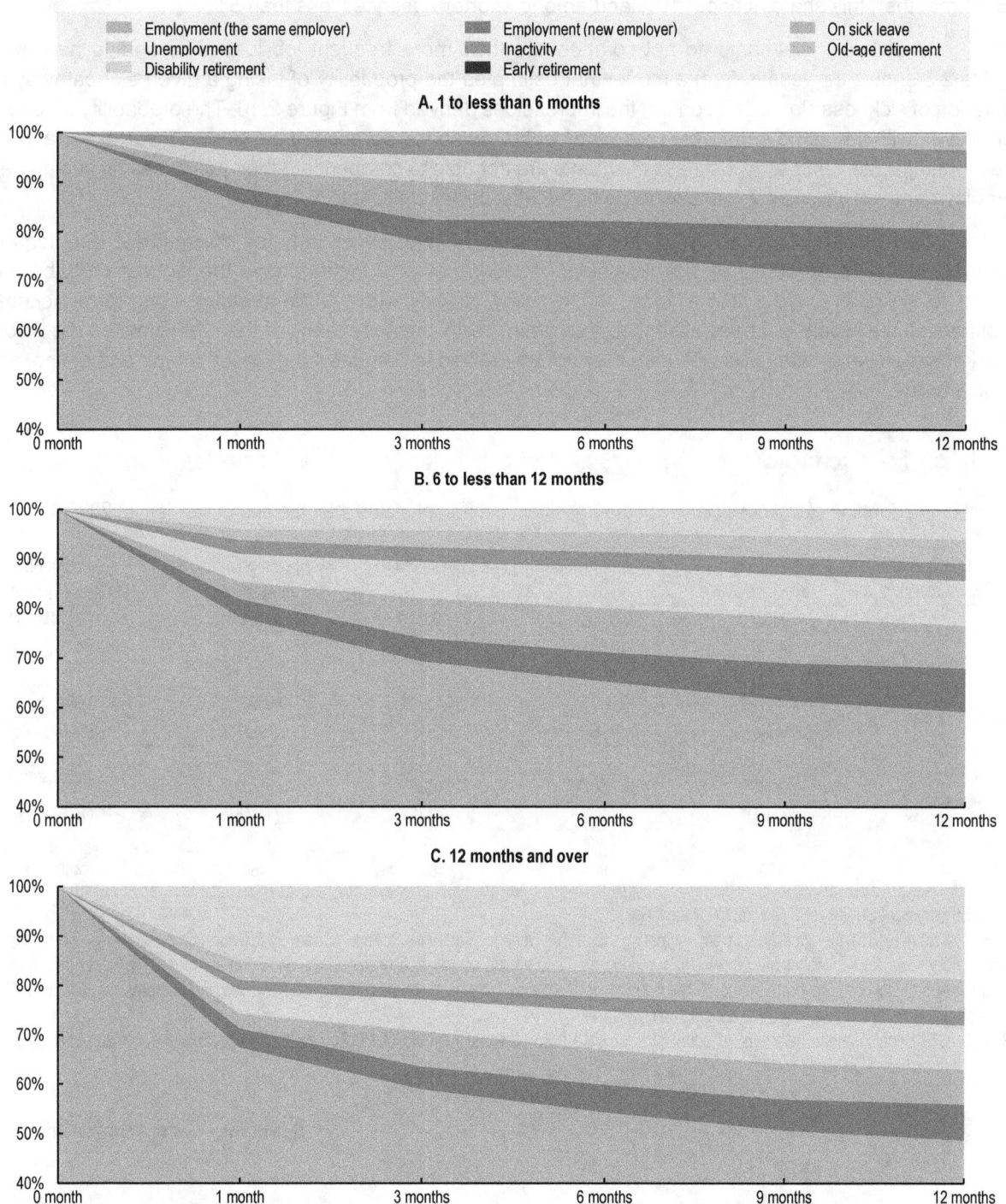

Note: At month 0, sickness claims are terminated and all employees are still employed (employment is a pre-condition for benefit receipt). Pathways follow ex-claimants for 12 months after termination of their claim. Include claims from mental health, cardiovascular disease, work injuries and diabetes (about 10% of all cases); they are indicative of the pathways but not representative.
Source: OECD calculations using administrative data from National Institute of Public Health (NIJZ), Employment Services Slovenia (ESS), Pension and Disability Insurance Institute Slovenia (ZPIZ).

StatLink https://stat.link/9xbg0q

Transitions from sickness to disability insurance are rare after short absence spells but quite frequent for those who have been absent from work for at least a year. Figure 2.10 shows that one year after the end of a long-term sickness absence, about 17% have retired via a disability and another 6% via an old-age pension; together almost one in four. Among sickness insurance claims of intermediate duration (6-12 months), this share is about 10% and among shorter absences less than 5%.

Long-term sickness claimants do not compensate their more frequent job losses by finding new jobs. Table 2.5 shows the results from a model that estimates the probability of taking a given exit pathway by duration of sickness claim, and confirm the impressions derived from Figure 2.10. The probability to remain employed with the same employers decreases notably with the duration of a sickness insurance claim, as described above. Long-term sickness claimants are not able to compensate their job losses by finding new employment, which Table 2.5 shows to be non-statistically significant.

There is a substantial probability to return to sickness leave, particularly for intermediate durations of sickness absence. People with sickness claim durations of 6-12 months have the highest probability to return to sickness leave within a year (and typically already within three months). Long-term sickness claimants have repeat sickness absences less often, partly because many of them have exited the labour market already and partly because they may not be entitled to benefits if they lost their job and did not find a new one.

Table 2.5. Long-term sickness claimants are more likely to return to sickness leave and to retire

Effect of the duration of sickness claims on the transition to different states after the end of sick leave, 2005-17

| Duration of sickness claim | Remaining employed | New employment | Sickness leave | Registration at ESS (jobseekers) | Retirement (DI and old-age) |
|---|---|---|---|---|---|
| 1-6 months | -0.0457*** | 0.00372 | 0.00931*** | 0.0195*** | 0.00824*** |
|  | (4.09) | (0.67) | (3.96) | (6.53) | (4.01) |
| 6<12 months | -0.161*** | -0.00045 | 0.0333*** | 0.0398*** | 0.057*** |
|  | (13.43) | (0.09) | (8.81) | (12.37) | (13.37) |
| 12+ months | -0.273*** | -0.00672 | 0.0180*** | 0.0365*** | 0.124*** |
|  | (23.01) | (1.32) | (5.73) | (11.45) | (18.64) |
| N | 460 | 460 | 460 | 460 | 460 |

ESS: Employment Service of Slovenia, DI: Disability.
Note: The table reports the coefficients from estimating the probability specified in the column header by the duration on sickness leave as main explanatory variable. T-statistics are reported in parentheses. Time effects accounting for transitions occurring at month 1, 3, 6, 9 and 12 months after the end of sickness leave are included. The figure includes claims from mental health, CVD, work injuries and diabetes only (about 10% of all cases); these results are indicative but not representative.
Source: OECD calculations using linked administrative data from National Institute of Public Health (NIJZ), Employment Services Slovenia (ESS), Pension and Disability Insurance Institute Slovenia (ZPIZ).

StatLink https://stat.link/g0quib

Older workers, low-skilled workers and those with low wages or a temporary contract are less able to keep their employment position after long periods of sick leave. Table 2.6 shows the differential effects of claim duration on the probability of employment (either in the same job or in a new job) by individual characteristics of claimants. Poor employment and poor skills largely decrease the probability to remain employed for long-term claimants to an extent that is greater than the severity of the health shock.

**Table 2.6. Accounting for the characteristics of claimants washes out some of the impacts of duration of sickness claims on the probability to remain employed**

Differences in the probability to stay employed across claimant characteristics, total 2005-17

|  | 6-12 months | 12+ months |
|---|---|---|
| Older vs Younger | -51% | -45% |
| p-value | <0.001 | <0.001 |
| Primary vs Secondary education | -40% | -32% |
| p-value | <0.001 | <0.001 |
| Women vs Men | 3.4% | 1.1% |
| p-value | 0.622 | 0.697 |
| Severe health shock vs no health shock | -31% | -8.7% |
| p-value | <0.001 | <0.001 |
| Temporary vs permanent contract | -80% | -41% |
| p-value | <0.001 | <0.001 |
| Lowest vs highest wage quintile | -42% | -31% |
| p-value | <0.001 | <0.001 |

Note: Differences are obtained by subtracting the employment effect for older (50-64) and younger (25-49), primary and secondary educational attainment, women and men, severe health shock (hospitalisation and medication in the past year) and no health shock, temporary and permanent contract, and lowest and highest wage quintile. This difference is divided by the effect of the reference category (older, primary education etc.). P-values result from a t-test assessing the differences in employment effects.
Source: OECD calculations using linked administrative data from National Institute of Public Health (NIJZ), Employment Services Slovenia (ESS), Pension and Disability Insurance Institute Slovenia (ZPIZ).

StatLink ⬛⬛ https://stat.link/8lk9wj

## References

Albreht, T. et al. (2016), *Health Systems in Transition: Slovenia (Vol. 18 No. 3 2016)*. [1]

EUROSTAT (n.d.), *Earnings - Labour Market (incl. LFS)*, 2021, https://ec.europa.eu/eurostat/web/labour-market/earnings (accessed on 4 November 2021). [4]

OECD (2015), *Fit Mind, Fit Job: From Evidence to Practice in Mental Health and Work*, Mental Health and Work, OECD Publishing, Paris, https://dx.doi.org/10.1787/9789264228283-en. [3]

ZZZS (2020), *Podatki o obveznem zdravstvenem zavarovanju*. [2]

ZZZS (2016), *Podatki o obveznem zdravstvenem zavarovanju*. [5]

## Notes

[1] For COVID-19 related sickness absences, this regulation is lifted temporarily.

[2] See: https://www.rtvslo.si/dostopno/zzzs-je-skoraj-petino-odlocb-o-dolgotrajni-bolniski-izdal-z-zamudo/511546.

[3] Figure 2.5 is based on data shared by the NIJZ, where sickness spells were pooled in pre-determined duration bins. Focusing on sickness spells of 45 calendar days or longer, which corresponds to the sickness spells entirely financed by the ZZZS through sickness insurance (30 working days).

[4] Figure 2.8 is constructed using linked administrative record of sickness and employment records, which contain only four types of qualifying causes: mental health diseases, cardiovascular diseases (CVD), diabetes, and work injuries. These causes are not representative of the stock of sickness claims as they together represent less than 10% of all spells, although probably considerably more for long-term spells. Results from the administrative records, although illustrative, should thus not be generalised to the Slovenian sickness insurance as a whole.

[5] While this is useful, it adds some noise into the approximations, as sick payments are calculated using the number of *working* days but the administrative data records *calendar* days of sick leave. To overcome this issue, one can estimate the number of working days using the information of working days and calendar days in a certain month: (number of calendar days absent in a month / number of days in a month) x number of working days.

[6] Table 2.4 presents only the median characteristics, but the share of 25-49 year-olds decreases with duration on sickness leave, while the share of 50-64 year-olds increases.

# 3 The challenges of the Slovenian disability insurance programme

Slovenia has one of the largest disability benefit caseloads in OECD countries: despite a gradual decline in the past 15 years, still almost one in ten people of working age receive a disability payment. This high share is surprising because the average payment is relatively low (not least due to considerable insurance requirements) and because disability insurance can turn away applicants with incomplete medical treatment and rehabilitation. Without the backlog for health treatments and without unlimited sickness insurance, the disability caseload would arguably be even larger. The system faces two major obstacles. First, it is complex and offers a number of different payments depending on age, degree of work capacity and eligibility for vocational rehabilitation. Second, vocational rehabilitation is built into the system but take-up is almost negligible because the support is coming too late. The system leaves many with very low payment and no return-to-work perspective. Only comprehensive reform can fix this.

Slovenia's disability insurance offers various benefits, depending on the result of the capacity assessment, including three types of disability benefits, a disability allowance, and a special benefit tied to vocational rehabilitation. Two particularities of the Slovenian disability insurance system are, first, that it covers both general disabilities and occupational injuries and diseases and, second, that employers play a key role at a time when workers will often have been out of work for a very long time. This section covers the main features of the programme, discusses the assessment of disability, including the coverage of occupational and non-work related disabilities, and wraps up by reviewing the co-operation (or rather the lack of it) between sickness and disability insurance.

## 3.1. Main characteristics of the programme

### 3.1.1. Benefit provision, funding and organisation

In Slovenia, disability insurance is contribution-based, covering those with substantial insurance periods gained through employment and self-employment. Insurance cover includes student work, farmers, and most forms of employment and self-employment. Non-eligible persons may join compulsory pension and disability insurance schemes on a voluntary basis.

Disability insurance is financed by contributions to the Pension and Disability Insurance Institute of Slovenia, ZPIZ. Social security contribution rates are 24.35% of the gross wage, of which employers pay 15.5% and employees 8.85%, and are used to cover old-age, disability and survivor insurance.[1] Like for health care spending, the strong reliance on social security contributions for financing makes the ZPIZ budget more sensitive to the economic cycle. Unlike for the ZZZS, the government is legally obliged to cover the gap between ZPIZ social security contributions and ZPIZ spending from the general budget (Stropnik, Prevolnik Rupel and Majcen, 2019[1]). This possibility effectively offers ZPIZ and disability insurance a greater flexibility than ZZZS and sickness insurance.

Other than social security contributions, employers have no additional costs to bear when their employees are on disability insurance. Unlike for sickness insurance, where employers pay for the first 30 working days of sickness, the costs of disability insurance for employers are limited to the mandatory social security contributions to ZPIZ. There are no financial consequences for having one, or many, employees on disability benefits. Employers, however, play a role in other ways in the concession of benefits, discussed in detail further below.

### 3.1.2. Coverage and generosity

Disability insurance covers all occupational and non-work injuries and diseases that cannot improve by continued medical treatment (MISSOC, 2021[2]). Benefit applicants not having completed their medical treatment, a condition not specified in the legal basis for benefit eligibility in most other EU or OECD countries, explain almost 60% of all benefit rejections in any given year.

Unemployed people can apply to the disability insurance programme without going through sickness insurance. Jobseekers registered at the ESS that are identified as facing employment barriers due to health limitations can apply for disability benefits directly (and also have to, as they are not entitled to sickness benefits), just as other inactive people with a sufficient insurance record.

The system is more lenient and generous for occupational injuries and diseases. Claimants with a work-related disability are entitled to disability insurance regardless of their contributory period. The minimum income replacement rate for these cases is set at 58.5% of the benefit base (see below for more details) for work histories shorter than 40 years, increasing with every year of contributions of over 40 years. This replacement rate for occupational injuries and diseases is almost twice the minimum replacement rate of the pension for non-work related disabilities and the minimum old age pension.

For non-occupational diseases and injuries, eligibility to disability insurance depends on the years of contributions to ZPIZ and the age of the claimant. For claimants under age 21, benefit entitlement requires at least three months of contributions. For this group, only full disability risks are covered, i.e. people can only receive a permanent disability pension (more on the type of benefits granted below). Claimants aged 21 to 29 must have employment for at least one-quarter of the time between the age of 21 and the occurrence of invalidity (full years of service). Claimants over age 30 must have employment for at least one-third of the time between age 20 and the occurrence of invalidity (only full years of service are considered). This system generates a discontinuity at age 21, and another at age 30, by which someone slightly younger than 30 is entitled to benefits with 2 years and 3 months of contributions, while someone having turned 30 requires 3 years and 4 months of contributions (see Figure 3.1).

Figure 3.1. Minimum years of contributions by age for disability insurance benefits eligibility

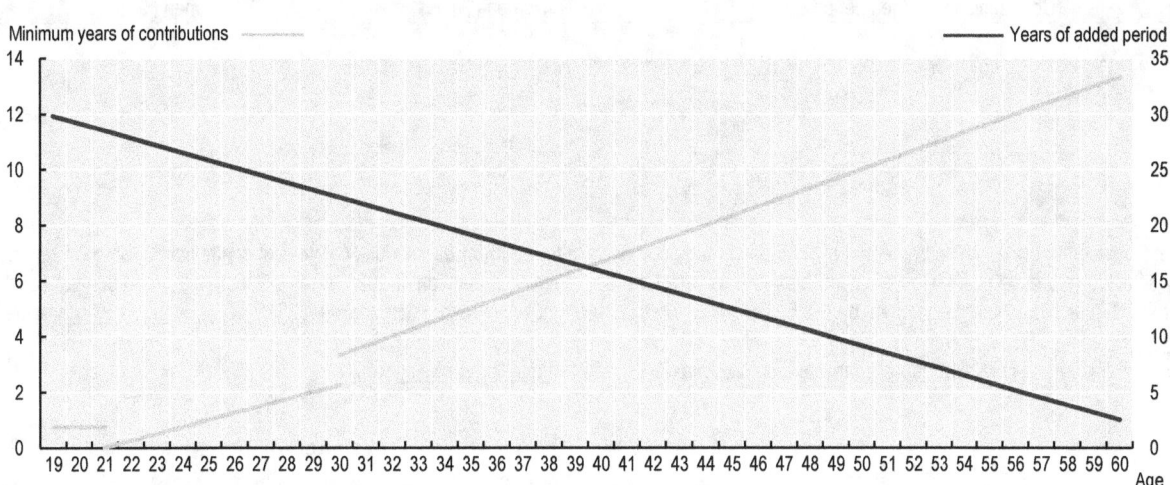

Note: For claimants under age 21, only full disability (category I) is covered, and so the only possible benefit being granted is a disability pension. The added period (prištete dobe) is a function of the age of disability onset, added to the number of years of contribution. The sum of the contributory years and the added period form the reference years, basis for calculating disability benefits.
Source: MISSOC (2020), https://www.missoc.org/.

StatLink ⫶ https://stat.link/wzxgyp

In addition to the reason for disability, benefit generosity depends on the years of contribution and on gender. For non-work related injuries, replacement rates from disability insurance follow the same pattern than old-age pensions: they increase with years of contributions, and are slightly different for men and women (see Table 3.1, although by 2023 the replacement rates should be equalised across gender). The pension basis over which the replacement rate is applied (PRB) is the monthly average of earnings in any consecutive 24-year period of insurance following 1 January 1970 (whichever is the most favourable for the insured person) (MISSOC, 2021[2]). Calculation of the PRB is based on earnings (net of taxes and other contributions) upon which pension contributions have been paid. To account for the foregone working years due to disability, the reference years used to determine the replacement rate are the sum of the contributory years and the *added period* (prištete dobe). The added period is a function of the age of disability onset ($a$) and calculated as:

$$Added\ Period = f(a) = \begin{cases} \frac{2}{3}(60-a) + \frac{1}{2}(65-60), a < 60 \\ \frac{1}{2}(65-a), 60 \leq a < 65 \end{cases}$$

The calculation of the *added period* adds a discontinuity at age 60, by slightly reducing the generosity in the calculation of disability pensions.

Pensions are higher if recipients have dependent children, according to Article 37 of the Act. For example, parents with 20 years of contributions and 13 years of added period and with two dependent children will receive a replacement rate of 56.7%, compared to 53.98% for the same situation without children. Having three children increases the benefit by 4 percentage points.

Table 3.1. Benefit generosity depends on the years of contribution and on gender

Replacement rate of disability and old age pension by contributory years and gender, 2020

| Key reference years (Contributions + added period) | Replacement rate women (%) | Replacement rate men (%) |
| --- | --- | --- |
| 15 | 29.5 | 27.0 |
| 20 | 36.3 | 33.3 |
| 25 | 43.1 | 39.6 |
| 30 | 49.9 | 45.9 |
| 35 | 56.7 | 52.2 |
| 40 | 63.5 | 58.5 |

Note: Replacement rates are incremented by 1.36 percentage points (1.26 for men) for each additional year of contribution. Table 2.1 reports only selected reference years. Replacement rates for men are for those claiming a pension in 2020; rates will increase proportionately each year, until matching those of women by 2025. For more details, see https://www.zpiz.si/cms/content2019/lestvice-za-odmero-starostne-pokojnine.
Source: Pension and Disability Insurance Institute of Slovenia (ZPIZ), 2021, https://www.zpiz.si/.

StatLink https://stat.link/76jlkr

The effective disability and old-age pension replacement rate has fallen steadily in the past decade (Figure 3.2). Disability pension entitlements follow the path set with any pension reform, which is a clear disadvantage of a disability insurance linked with pension insurance as pension eligibility conditions worsen, especially in a situation in which disability benefit payments are relatively low. From 2010 to 2017, net disability pension entitlements fell by about 14%, from 51.8% of net earnings to 45%, largely owing to the gradual extension of the earnings period considered for the calculation of pensions entitlements. Since 2017, payments remained largely unchanged.

Depending on their disability assessment, claimants may be entitled to a disability pension, a disability benefit, or a part-time benefit. A disability pension is granted to eligible claimants who cannot be employed due to very severe disabilities and old age, and meet the minimum contribution requirements. A disability benefit is granted to persons with residual employment capacity who cannot work at their current job but could potentially work elsewhere (right to transfer, *pravica do premestitve*). A part-time disability benefit is granted to claimants who can no longer work full-time.

Vocational rehabilitation can be granted instead of the right to transfer to another job or a partial disability benefit. As an alternative outcome after a disability assessment, vocational rehabilitation can be granted to younger claimants (under age 55) who have remaining work capacity and the potential to be trained for another job on a full-time (if age 50-54) or part-time basis (if under age 50 years). Vocational rehabilitation is thus granted on a sufficient residual work capacity, Category II of disability, which will be described in more detail below.

**Figure 3.2. Due to pension reform, disability pension entitlements dropped by about 14%**

Ratio between net average pension payments and net average earnings for both disability and old age pensions, over time

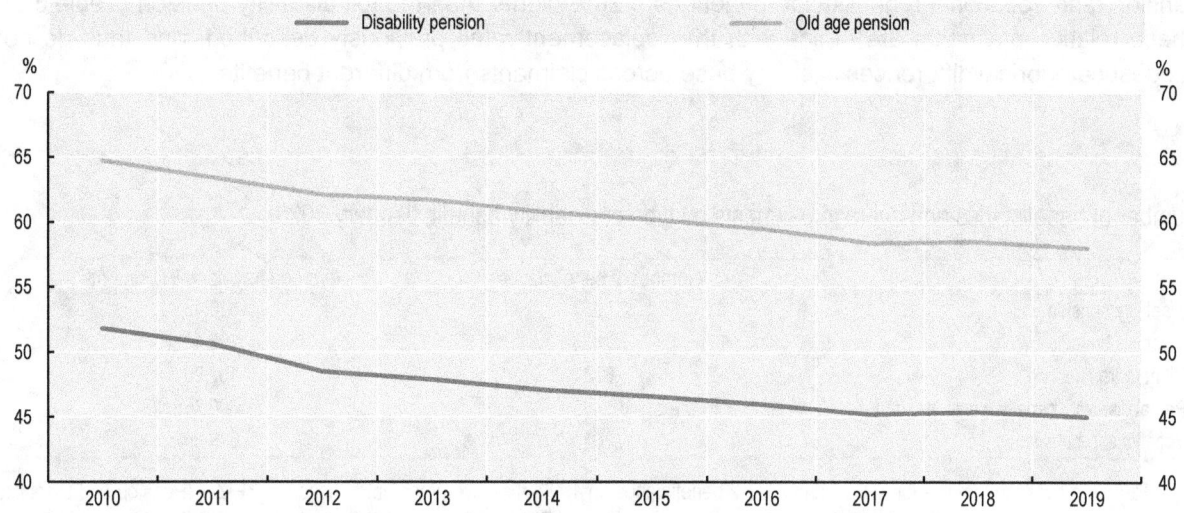

Source: ZPIZ (2020), Mesečni statistični pregled januar 2020, www.zpiz.si/cms/userfiles/file/MSP_januar_2020.pdf.

StatLink ⟶ https://stat.link/9zj0oy

All benefits are calculated relative to the disability pension. As shown in Figure 3.3, the calculation of the *added period* adds a discontinuity at age 60, by slightly reducing the generosity in the calculation of disability benefits. This is common practice in many countries – assuming that people would not have worked until the legal retirement age – but further reducing benefit entitlements unnecessarily. From this basis, entitlements for the various disability benefits are as follows:

- Full disability benefits pay 60% or 80% of the disability pension, depending on the residual work capacity. These amounts are only paid to claimants who are not employed but for whom the cause of non-employment is involuntary; claimants having terminated their employment contract voluntarily receive only 25% or 40% of the disability pension.
- Disability claimants with the right to transfer having started another job receive 20% or 35% of the disability pension. In addition to partial benefits, this is another form of financial incentive to work in the Slovenian disability insurance system. Its efficacy is not clear, however, since claimants with more residual employment capacity receive a higher pay (35% of the disability pension) than those assessed as having less residual employment capacity (20%).
- Partial benefits are calculated as a proportional reduction of the disability pension as working hours increase. Claimants working 20 hours a week will receive 50% of the pension, and those working 35 hours receive 12.5%. The proportional reduction in hours worked results in limited incentives to increase working hours. Unemployed workers assessed as having sufficient capacity to work part-time receive 80% of the disability pension.
- Claimants in vocational rehabilitation are entitled to a benefit 30% higher than the corresponding disability pension, for the period from the acquisition of the right to the completion of vocational rehabilitation. Those only engaged in part-time vocational rehabilitation receive 40% of the disability pension. After completion of vocational rehabilitation, employed claimants receive benefit levels as previously described. Unemployed claimants receive 50% of the pension until finding employment, for a maximum of two years.

In 2020, the average disability benefit paid 38% of the average disability pension. This suggests a substantial number of voluntarily unemployed claimants, or a lower salary base for recipients of disability benefits than that of pension recipients. Benefits granted for the right to transfer are about 30% the average disability pension (replacement rate is 20-35%), partial payments amount to 60% of the full disability pension, and vocational rehabilitation benefits are 20% higher than the full disability pension (Table 3.2). These relative payments are in line with the replacement rates previously described, and thus do not suggest categorical differences in salary base across claimants from different benefits.

Table 3.2. The average disability benefit paid amounts to 38% of the average disability pension paid

Number of beneficiaries and average payments by type of disability benefit, January 2020

|  | Number of beneficiaries | Average payment, EUR/month |
| --- | --- | --- |
| Disability pension | 77 361 | 516,43 |
| Disability benefits | 18 833 | 198,40 |
| Right to transfer | 623 | 152,20 |
| Partial disability benefits/pension | 15.497 | 306,75 |
| Vocational rehabilitation | 206 | 619,95 |

Note: Reported average benefits for ZPIZ-1 and ZPIZ-2 beneficiaries. In 1999, the government introduced the ZPIZ-1 (Pension and Disability Insurance Act). The third amendment to the legislation, the new Pension and Disability Insurance Act (hereinafter: ZPIZ-2, entered into force on 1 January 2013. Average benefits are virtually unchanged from December 2019.
Source: ZPIZ (2020), Mesečni statistični pregled januar 2020, https://www.zpiz.si/cms/userfiles/file/MSP_januar_2020.pdf.

StatLink ⏩ https://stat.link/lqn3r0

Upon reaching retirement age, disability pension beneficiaries do not switch to the old-age pension programme, as people are granted permanent rights to a disability pension (until their death).[2] This is because disability pensions are calculated on the same basis than old-age pensions, and thus effectively the transition to retirement age does not result in a change in benefit for pensioners. This anomaly, however, can make cross-country comparisons for persons older than 65 more difficult.

### 3.2. Assessment of disability benefits

#### 3.2.1. The process of receiving disability benefits

The process of receiving disability benefits usually starts with a request to the ZPIZ from the insured worker, the GP, or the occupational medicine expert at the request of the GP. In most cases, the personal GP initiates the process of application for disability insurance payments by requesting a disability assessment at the ZPIZ Disability Commission. However, employers or workers themselves can also start the process. Regardless of who initiates the process, personal GPs are responsible for completing the standardised medical form that forms the base for the application to disability insurance.

ZZZS physicians play a minor role in the application to ZPIZ, as they only propose applications for consideration to ZPIZ. For instance, after one year of sickness absence, ZZZS physicians suggest their beneficiaries for disability assessment. Yet, ZZZS experts claim that this is a formality, which often results in a rejection of the application from ZPIZ on the grounds of incomplete medical treatment.

After receipt of the medical information, employers and insured persons are requested to provide working documentation, *delovno dokumentacijo*, which assesses the burdens of the job performed and the skills of the insured person, and evaluates the possibility for vocational rehabilitation. These work information forms, DD-1, DD-2, DD-3, DD-2 MZ (see Appendix for the forms and their English translation), are instrumental for disability assessment by the ZPIZ Disability Commission. In the case of an unemployed insured person, the Employment Service of Slovenia (ESS) is responsible for submitting the relevant work information forms.

Insured persons and their employers decide whether to exercise their right of vocational rehabilitation. In Slovenia, vocational rehabilitation is granted with the purpose to continue employment with the same employer, by adapting the current job or taking up a different position in the same company. The disability commission proposes the participation to vocational rehabilitation on grounds of the medical and working information. Both the employer and the insured persons must agree to exercise this right, by a formal statement of their wish to rehabilitate professionally. Only then the insured person is referred to a professional institution in the field of occupational medicine or vocational rehabilitation, which gives an opinion on the cursus of vocational rehabilitation.

In theory, the deadline for ZPIZ for issuing a decision is four months, but de facto, the process takes twice as long. The process to apply for disability insurance payments starts when all documentation is completed. From that moment on, ZPIZ specialists have four months to complete their assessment. However, Table 3.3 shows that in reality the process takes about eight months on average (slightly shorter for a partial benefit); this could be a deterrent for some potentially eligible people to apply to the disability insurance programme (Autor, Duggan and Gruber, 2014[3]).

Table 3.3. Average waiting time between the application to the programme and benefit receipt

Average duration of procedures by type of application, I-XII 2019

|  | Disability pension | Disability benefit |
| --- | --- | --- |
|  | Number of days | Number of days |
| Preparatory procedure before disability assessment (IK assessment) | 53 | 53 |
| Classification according to IK assessment | 134 | 134 |
| Granting benefits | 67 | 44 |
| **TOTAL** | **254** | **231** |

Source: Data shared by the Pension and Disability Insurance Institute of Slovenia (ZPIZ) www.zpiz.si.

StatLink https://stat.link/26nvle

### The assessment of disability

A key aspect of eligibility for disability insurance benefits is that the applicant must have a disability that cannot be improved by medical treatment or rehabilitation. The starting point for the assessment of disability is a medical assessment. ZPIZ physicians assess the medical form provided by applicants, and completed by their GP, following the ICD-10 criteria for limitations of work capacity in relation to a medical condition, not taking into account capacity for the actual job performed. Once it is established that no improvement is possible through medical rehabilitation, the Disability Commission determines the remaining work capacity of the applicant.

Over half of the rejections from disability insurance are due to uncompleted medical treatment. The condition that disability cannot be improved by medical treatment or rehabilitation is binding. Figure 3.3 below decomposes the first-instance disability-assessment decisions between acceptances to the programme, rejections due to insufficient degree of disability, and rejections due to incomplete medical treatment. In 2019, 26% of all applicants were not accepted in the programme in the first instance, a share that is quite stable over time and lower than in most other EU and OECD countries, except the Nordics

(OECD, 2010[4]). Out of all rejections, 56% were rejected because the medical treatment was considered incomplete, a share that has slightly increased in recent years.

Figure 3.3. Over half of the disability insurance rejections are due to incomplete medical treatment

Composition of first instance ZPIZ decisions regarding disability insurance, disaggregated by acceptance, rejection due to no disability and rejection due to incomplete medical treatment, 2019

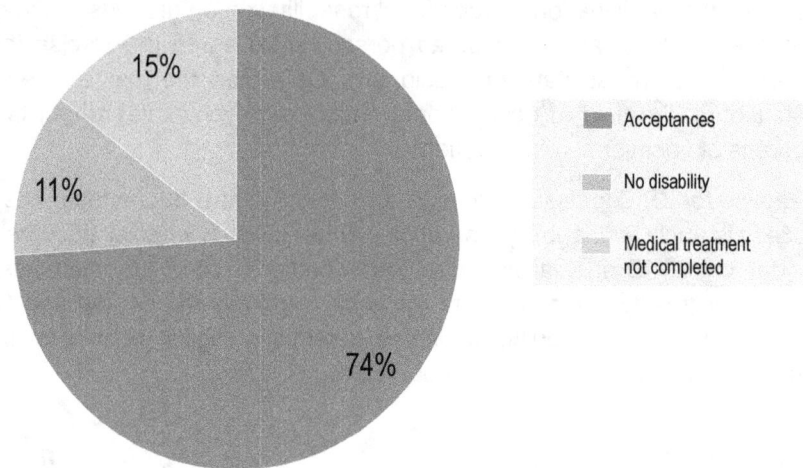

Source: OECD calculations based on data from the Pension and Disability Insurance Institute of Slovenia (ZPIZ) www.zpiz.si.

StatLink https://stat.link/2n15mp

Applicants with full disability undergo a medical assessment only, without an assessment of their employment capacity. Applicants who are found not to be able to work for more than four hours per week for medical reasons (complete incapacity for work, or occupational incapacity for work without remaining working capacity) do not have their work capacity assessed. They are directly classified as fully disabled (Category I of disability), with entitlement to a disability pension. This presents a certain inconsistency as the inability to work at least four hours per week is determined by ZPIZ caseworkers on the basis of a medical assessment only, e.g. without accounting for the characteristics of their previous job or occupation.

All remaining applicants undergo an in-depth assessment of their working capacity. For this capacity assessment, the employer and the insured worker have to provide information on the nature, the workload, and the burden of the occupation/job through a standardised form. The assessment is based on workload and burden (physical demand) in both theory and practice, i.e. of the job position and of the work done by the insured person. Depending on the assessed capacity, eligible applicants are classified into one of two additional categories:

- Category II, if the working capacity is reduced by 50% or more, or the person is no longer capable of working in the current profession (de facto often equated with "the current job");
- Category III, when working capacity is reduced by less than 50%, but working for at least half of the working hours is not possible or the person is no longer capable of working at the current place of employment.

The decision to grant the right to vocational rehabilitation on the same work capacity assessment and on the person's age. Vocational rehabilitation is *mandatory* for all applicants under age 50 classified under disability Category II (or, under age 55 and able to work part-time). People aged 55 or older classified in

Category II, and all applicants classified in Category III, have an *optional* right to vocational rehabilitation. No additional assessments take place.

Slovenia's disability assessment reflects a rather unique application of the principles of the ICF. For persons with full disability, assessment is largely medical as it is "assumed" that the person has no remaining capacity that could be used in the labour market. For all other workers, disability is assessed by comparing the person's current capacity with the demands of the previous occupation or, de facto, the last job; the estimated potential number of hours the applicant could work determines the category of disability. The degree of disability is strongly influenced by two factors: the education and occupation of the applicant and the work environment in the last job. This is a promising approach in theory but not in practice because this comparison is, in most cases, only done years after the applicant has left her or his job. Moreover, the process and its outcome relies heavily on the ability and willingness of the employer and the applicant to provide the necessary information and to co-operate in vocational rehabilitation.

The disability insurance system is complex and admits preferential treatment for workers above age 50. Figure 3.4 summarises the application process to ZPIZ benefits or rights, which depends on the severity of the work limitation but also age. Workers above age 50, who could regain work capacity if undergoing vocational rehabilitation, can qualify for a permanent disability pension. Similarly, workers above age 55 can be eligible for a permanent disability benefit despite remaining work capacity, while those younger than age 55 can only receive a temporary disability benefit (Fialho and Høj, 2020[5]).

Figure 3.4. The disability insurance system is complex and admits preferential treatment for workers above age 50

Application process to ZPIZ

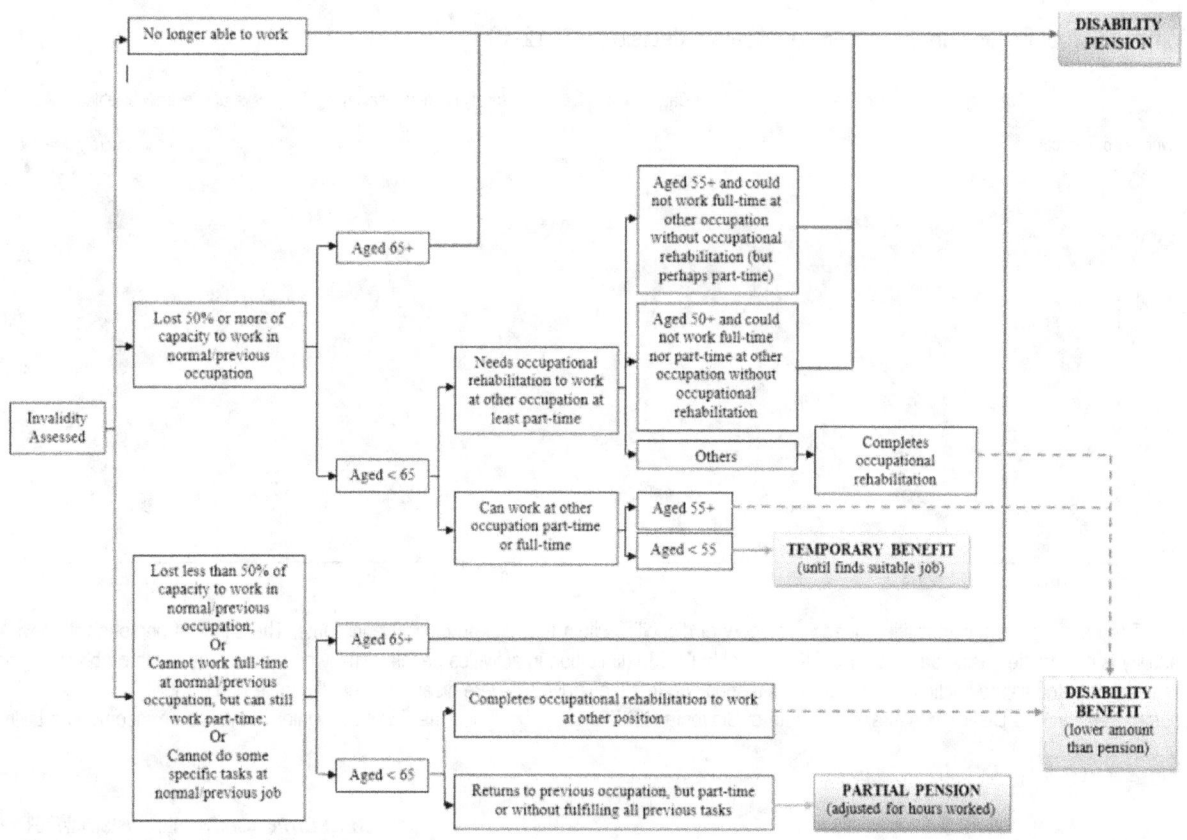

Source: Fialho, P. and J. Høj (2020), "Labour market institutions for an ageing labour force in Slovenia", *OECD Economics Department Working Papers*, No. 1 648, https://doi.org/10.1787/9eca1535-en.

The large majority of new applicants in Slovenia are categorised into the "lightest" category of disability. Figure 3.5 shows that, in 2019, almost 70% of all applicants are classified as Category III of disability after their initial disability assessment. Category II represent 8%, Category I represent 16%, and the remaining 7% are referred to vocational rehabilitation. While the share of applicants initially classified as Category III of disability is constant over time, the composition of first-instance decisions has seen an increase in referrals to vocational rehabilitation and Category II of disability, at the expense of Category I. It could be that the composition of applicants has changed, towards persons with more residual employment capacity. This is in line with the trend in the share of persons with severe disability identified in population surveys, as shown in Figure 3.5, except for 2019, where survey data show a sudden increase in the prevalence of severe disability. A mutually non-exclusive alternative explanation is that this is the result of a change in the culture or practice of disability assessments. This would be a step in the right direction, as it implies granting fewer permanent disability pensions, and more disability benefits, which have an activation component.

De facto, there is some room for interpretation on the process of granting rights to vocational rehabilitation. Applicants and employers play a big role in deciding whether to participate in vocational rehabilitation, even in the cases where participation should be mandatory. Disability applicants often prefer to be classified in Category III of disability, with a lower benefit entitlement, and have the right to opt out of rehabilitation benefits. Employers can argue for the unavailability of jobs that the claimant could perform in spite of undergoing vocational rehabilitation. Since there is such as close tie between disability assessment and the job before disability onset, employers' lack of commitment is sufficient to refuse the right to vocational rehabilitation.

**Figure 3.5. The large majority of applicants are categorised as the lightest category of disability**

Composition of first instance disability application decisions, 2012-19

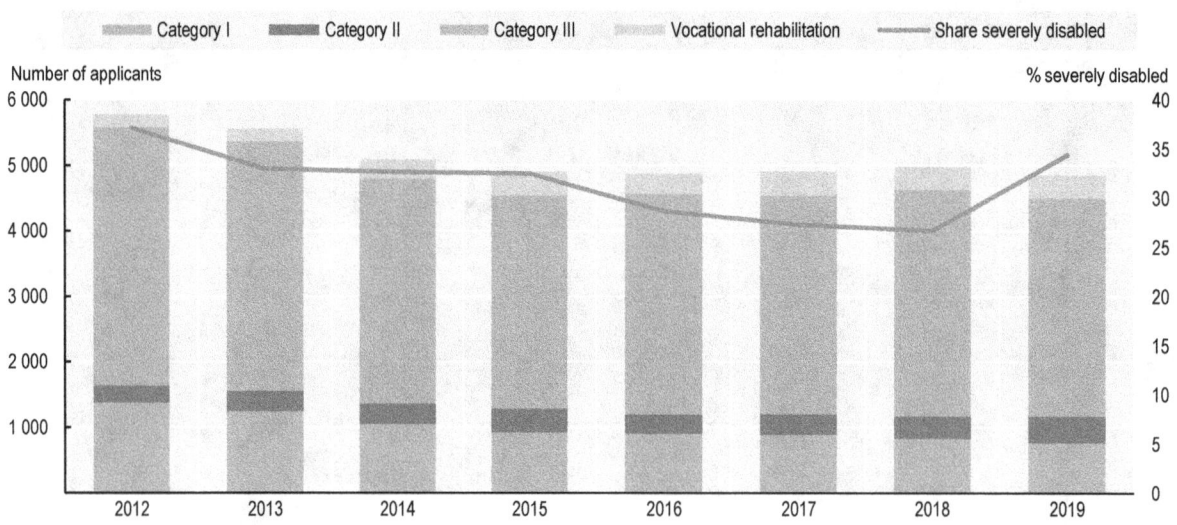

Note: The bars show the composition of each category of disability within the total number of applicants. The share of persons with severe disability is constructed using data from EU-SILC (variable PH030 (limitation in activities people usually do because of health problems)). The share is calculated as the fraction of those persons responding that they have a severe disability over all people with disability.
Source: Pension and Disability Insurance Institute of Slovenia (ZPIZ) www.zpiz.si/ and the European Union Statistics on Income and Living Conditions (EU-SILC).

StatLink https://stat.link/26keou

Despite an increase in the rate of referral to vocational rehabilitation, the number of disability applicants engaging in it remains low. Figure 3.5 shows a slight increase of referrals to vocational rehabilitation. De facto, however, because there is so much room for interpretation, the take up of vocational rehabilitation remains low. Figure 3.6 shows that the number of new vocational rehabilitation contracts has remained rather constant over time (with two peaks, in 2015 and 2019), while the number of referrals to vocational rehabilitation has increased steadily (again, with an exception for 2015, a particularly proliferous year). The leeway given to employers and employees to decide whether to engage in vocational rehabilitation or not results in even lower actual take up.

The theoretical criteria to assess disability presents inconsistencies, compounded by a conflicting execution of the assessment. One theoretical inconsistency is the fact that qualification for Category I of disability requires applicants to be able to work less than four hours per week, while Category II requires a reduction of at least 50% of the working capacity. In theory, working capacity is assessed against the current profession, while de facto only the previous job is taken into account. For unemployed workers, the assessment refers to the last job before unemployment. This is despite of the latest legislative reform in 2013, which attempted to broaden the definition of work capacity to consider the applicants' profession. This mismatch between theory and practice makes it difficult to evaluate the assessment of disability and to provide recommendations. Another conflicting aspect, exemplified above, is that while vocational rehabilitation is a right that should be mandatory, there is a lot of room for never taking it up. Relatedly, another limitation of the system is activation for disability applicants and beneficiaries is tailored to remaining employed with the same employer. This is made worse by the fact that employers have a window of opportunity to fire their employees when they are granted disability benefits. Since this is a commonly used practice (see below in Chapter 2), it makes all the activation efforts redundant.

Figure 3.6. Despite a modest increase in the rate of referral to vocational rehabilitation, the number of disability applicants engaging in it remains low

Number of new vocational rehabilitation contracts in each year, compared to total number of participants, 2012-19

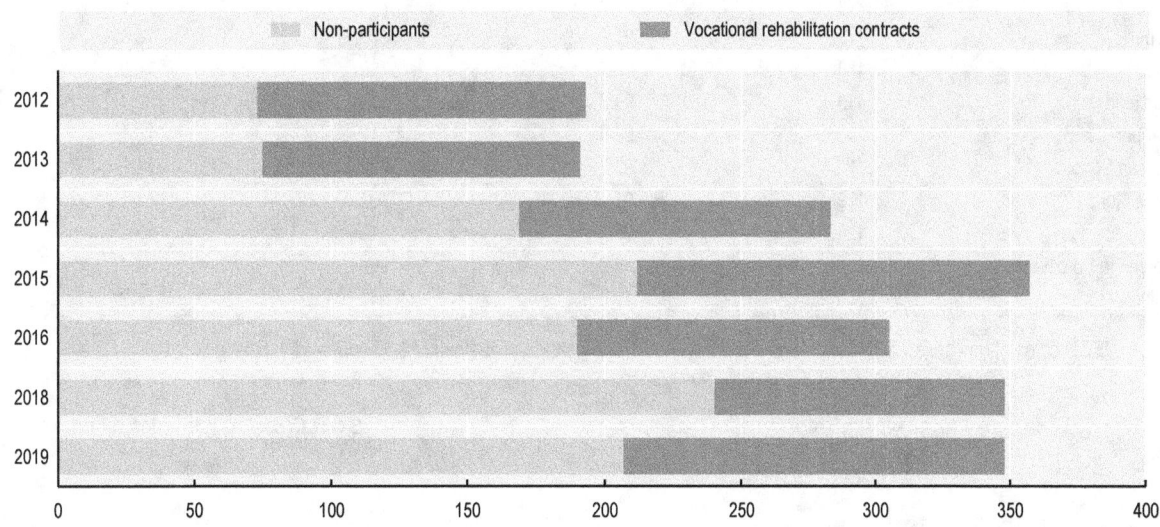

Note: Non-participants are constructed by subtracting the number of new contracts in a given year from the number of applicants referred to vocational rehabilitation. The assumption is that this subtraction is a proxy for claimants refusing to engage in vocational rehabilitation, as backlog in the decision is not a major issue. There are no data on the number of vocational rehabilitation contracts for 2017.
Source: Pension and Disability Insurance Institute of Slovenia (ZPIZ) www.zpiz.si/.

StatLink https://stat.link/pej02n

Work capacity assessments do not take into account economic conditions, nor the availability of vacancies in the job used to measure work capacity. A common complaint voiced by social partners is that the assessment of disability is based on unrealistic job possibilities, resulting in overly strict assessments. Taking into account the actual availability of the jobs that a claimant could perform in theory is a way to bridge these elements. Slovenian authorities may want to take as an example the Dutch disability assessment process, where residual earnings capacity is evaluated against all jobs that applicants could still perform given their medical, occupational and individual characteristics, for which there are at least three vacancies at the time of assessment.

The appeal process reverses the decision of the disability commission in about one in every four times. Figure 3.3 showed that about 26% of applicants were rejected in the first decision. The appeal process reverses about one-quarter of these decisions, leaving a final rejection rate of about 20%. ZPIZ is not in the position to share more in-depth data on the outcomes of appeals but anecdotal evidence from social partners seems to suggest that appeals are rarely successful, except in cases where ZPIZ did an obvious mistake.

The acceptance rate for disability pensions is significantly higher than for disability benefits, and with a lower regional variance. The national acceptance rate for applicants to disability pensions is 93%, while it is 77% for disability benefits (Table 3.4). While the acceptance rate for disability pensions fluctuates around 90% (with an exception for Novo Mesto, with almost 97%), the acceptance rate for disability benefits ranges from 71.5% in Celje to 84% in Novo Mesto.

Table 3.4. The acceptance rate for disability pensions is significantly higher than for disability benefits, and with lower regional variance

Number of applicants by type of benefit and region and acceptance rate to the programmes, 2019

|  | Applications disability pension | Acceptance rate (%) | Applications disability benefit | Acceptance rate (%) |
| --- | --- | --- | --- | --- |
| Celje | 274 | 92.3 | 1 773 | 71.5 |
| Koper | 72 | 91.7 | 531 | 73.4 |
| Kranj | 188 | 94.7 | 789 | 75.0 |
| Ljubljana | 413 | 90.8 | 1 558 | 80.4 |
| Maribor | 363 | 93.9 | 1 812 | 75.1 |
| Murska Sobota | 117 | 93.2 | 783 | 78.7 |
| Nova Gorica | 179 | 91.1 | 702 | 81.1 |
| Novo Mesto | 128 | 96.9 | 816 | 83.7 |
| Ravne na Koroškem | 129 | 89.9 | 902 | 81.4 |
| Total | 1 863 | 92.6 | 9 666 | 77.2 |

Source: OECD calculations based on Pension and Disability Insurance Institute of Slovenia (ZPIZ) data www.zpiz.si/.

StatLink https://stat.link/97p8ik

### 3.2.2. Disability reassessment

The process of reassessment of disability is the same as the initial assessment of disability. Reassessments take into account the current state of health of applicants, and its impact on their ability to work, just as with the initial assessment of disability. As such, reassessments do not take into account labour market changes and economic conditions, and heavily focus on assessing the residual working capacity against the previous job held by the person many years ago. For people who have entered the system when young and who have to undergo several rounds of reassessments, assessing against the previously held job only (or, in theory, the previous occupation) is a rather narrow approach.

Reassessments are less strict for older workers, adding to the incentives of older workers to take up disability insurance benefits. Reassessments are only periodically conducted (every five years) for claimants acquiring the right to benefits before the age of 45. In all other cases, ZPIZ specialists can request the reassessment of a case upon suspicion of abuse of acquired rights. Disability beneficiaries called in for reassessment are obliged to undergo a reassessment, and cannot influence the process. For claimants whose health status has improved to such an extent that they disqualify from the programme, benefits are paid for up to one month after the decision.

## 3.3. Descriptive statistics of the programme: Take up, average benefit payments, and outflows

Slovenia has one of the highest disability benefit recipiency rates in OECD countries, but it has decreased over the past decade. In Slovenia, almost 1 in 10 working age adults receive social support for their disability, one-third of these receiving a disability benefit, and the remainer a disability pension. This situates Slovenia as one of the OECD country with the highest disability support receipt rate, after Estonia, Lithuania and Norway. This high share is in a downward trend over the past decade, but caution is needed when interpreting this trend: most of the decling in ZPIZ receipt rates is captured by an increase in long-term sickness absences. What Slovenia is observing over the past decade is a long-term sickness issue, masking (among others) a large disability dependency issue. Comparing the generosity of the sickness sytem to that of the disability system, the spillovers from disability to sickness are not surprising.

Figure 3.7. Slovenia has one of the highest disability benefit recipiency rates in OECD countries, but it has decreased over the past decade

Disability benefit receipt rate in 2007 and 2018 in OECD countries

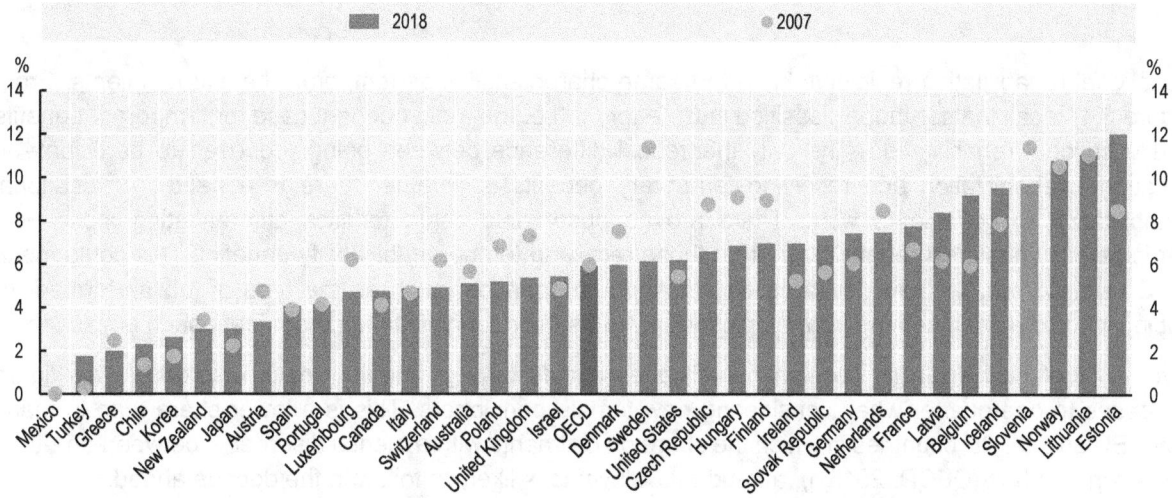

Note: Disability benefit receipt over population aged 20-64. Disability benefits include contributory and non-contributory programmes specifically targeted to persons with disability. OECD is an unweighted average excluding Colombia and Costa Rica. Data for 2018 refer to 2016 for Estonia, Italy and the United States. For Canada, data include federal insurance as well as provincial assistance benefits.
Source: OECD SOCR database https://www.oecd.org/s ocial/social-benefit-recipients-database.htm.

The representative disability pensioner is a man, enters the programme at age 50-54 with 25-34 years of contributions, and qualifies through a non-occupational disease for a Category I benefit. The same is true for the representative disability benefit recipient. Women are more often partial disability pensioners than men, but the median partial disability recipient otherwise enters the programme at the same age and with the same contributory periods than full disability pensioners. Temporary benefits are granted to those younger than 55, and so the representative recipient enters the programme at age 30-39, with four to 15 years of contributions. Across benefits, the most frequent qualifying disability is a non-occupational disease. Disability pensioners are mainly classified in the category of most severe disability (I), while disability benefit and partial disability recipients classify in the least severe disability category (III). Recipients of temporary benefits most often qualify in Category II. Table 3.5 summarises this information.

Table 3.5. The representative disability benefit recipient is a man, entering at age 50-54 with 25-34 years of contributions, and qualifying for a category I payment through a non-occupational disease

Most frequent characteristics of recipients (representative recipient) by benefit type, 2019

|  | Disability pension | (%) | Disability benefit | (%) | Partial disability | (%) | Temporary benefit | (%) | Vocational rehabilitation | (%) |
| --- | --- | --- | --- | --- | --- | --- | --- | --- | --- | --- |
| Gender | Man | 60 | Man | 56 | Woman | 64 | Man | 66 | Man | 61 |
| Age at entry in programme | 50-54 | 30 | 50-54 | 27 | 50-54 | 28 | 35-39 | 26 | 35-39 | 29 |
| Years of contributions | 25-34 | 46 | 25-34 | 40 | 25-34 | 46 | 5-14 | 47 | 5-14 | 52 |
| Qualifying disability | Disease | 93 | Disease | 83 | Disease | 93 | Disease | 62 | Disease | 74 |
| Category of disability | I | 88 | III | 98 | III | 100 | II | 70 | II | 69 |

Note: The table reports the most frequent characteristics of recipients by benefit type. Percentages (%) indicate the frequency with which this characteristics occur.
Source: OECD calculations based on Pension and Disability Insurance Institute of Slovenia (ZPIZ) data www.zpiz.si/.

StatLink https://stat.link/m036w2

Vocational rehabilitation recipients have the same characteristics as temporary benefit recipients. From Figure 3.4, recall that for those classified in Category II (i.e. the most frequent case for temporary benefits and vocational rehabilitation), the only theoretical difference between being proposed to participate in vocational rehabilitation and receiving temporary benefits is whether there is a need for vocational rehabilitation to be able to work. There are no observable characteristics differentiating those who participate in vocational rehabilitation from those receiving temporary disability benefits. This could mean ZPIZ assessors base their decisions on additional information, such as the type of job performed, or subjective information coming from employers, such as their capacity to accommodate such employee.

Over 18% of new disability pension beneficiaries qualify through mental health disorders. This figure increases to one-quarter when considering new female pensioners. This is a lower share than in many other EU and OECD countries in which the share on claimants with a mental disorder is between one-third and even one-half (OECD, 2015[6]), a trend that Slovenia is likely to follow in the decade ahead.

Disability pensions are low, often falling below the level of the Basic Minimum Income (*osnovni znesek minimalnega dohodka*). Data show that 80% of all disability pensions fall in a range between EUR 300 and EUR 800 per month, with a median of EUR 500 to EUR 600 (Figure 3.8). While this amount may be sufficient to secure a dignified living for those receiving a pension above the median, recipients in the low-earnings range, receive dangerously low payments. For comparison, over 22% of pension beneficiaries receive a pension below EUR 400, the threshold set for the Basic Minimum Income. The low level of pensions has been an issue raised by the Commission of the National Council for Social Welfare, Labour, Health and the Disabled, and assessed by the MoLFSA, over spring 2020.

Figure 3.8. Disability pensions are low, often falling below the Basic Minimum Income

Benefit level distributions by benefit type, 2019

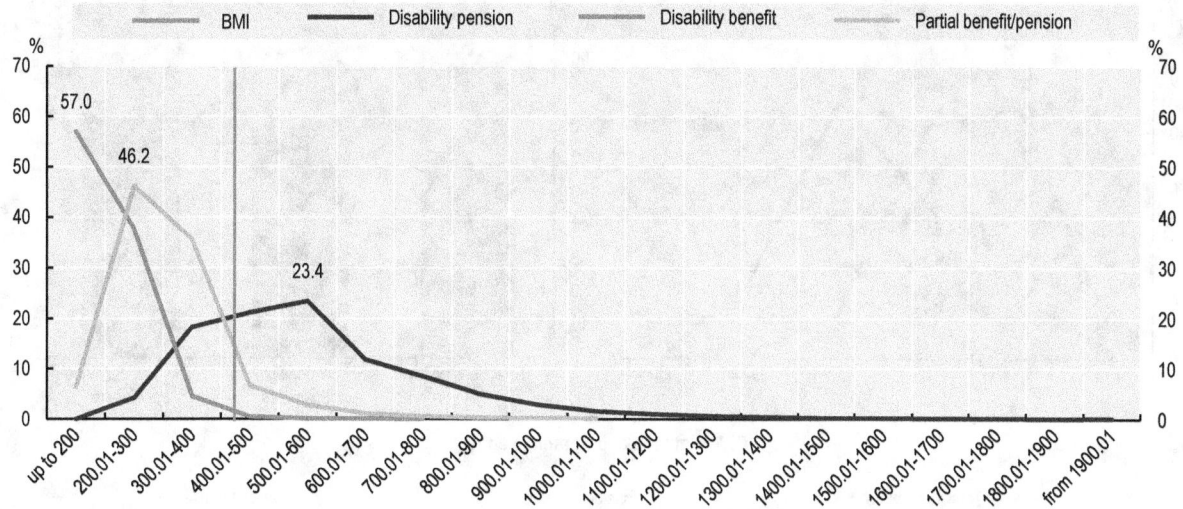

Notes: Basic Minimum Income (BMI) is EUR 402.18 per month.
Source: OECD calculations based on Pension and Disability Insurance Institute of Slovenia (ZPIZ) data www.zpiz.si/.

StatLink https://stat.link/hoj349

Short contributory periods are the key characteristic of recipients of low disability pensions. Figure 3.9 shows that recipients of pensions below EUR 400 (low pensions) and EUR 300 (very low pensions) mainly differ from the total pensioners by their insurance periods, which are substantially shorter. Again, this is a key weakness of many pensions-like disability insurance schemes compared to other systems, which only take the most recent earning into account or are unrelated to the person's level of earnings. Shorter insurance periods correlate with shorter labour market histories, and possibly lower labour market attachment and earnings, which could explain the lower pensions. Pensioners with low pensions are slightly younger than the average pensioner while those receiving very low pensions are somewhat older, indicating that age may not be the underlying factor behind low pensions.

Disability benefits, on which people stay on average for about six years, are clearly insufficient to sustain basic living expenses. Most disability beneficiaries (57%) receive less than EUR 200 per month in benefits (Figure 3.8). The potential rationale for such a low benefit is to provide incentives to look for a job quickly, being granted to those having completed vocational rehabilitation, or able to work part-time or full-time in another occupation. Disability benefits are a standalone income support, as it is not possible to combine them with earnings from work (only partial benefits can). The reality, however, is that claimants stay on disability benefits for about six years (five years for women) (Table 3.6). The level of disability benefits, thus, does not align with the reality of the job market persons with disability face.

## Figure 3.9. Short contributory periods are a key characteristic for low disability pensions

Characteristics of total pensioners compared to recipients of low and very low pensions, 2019

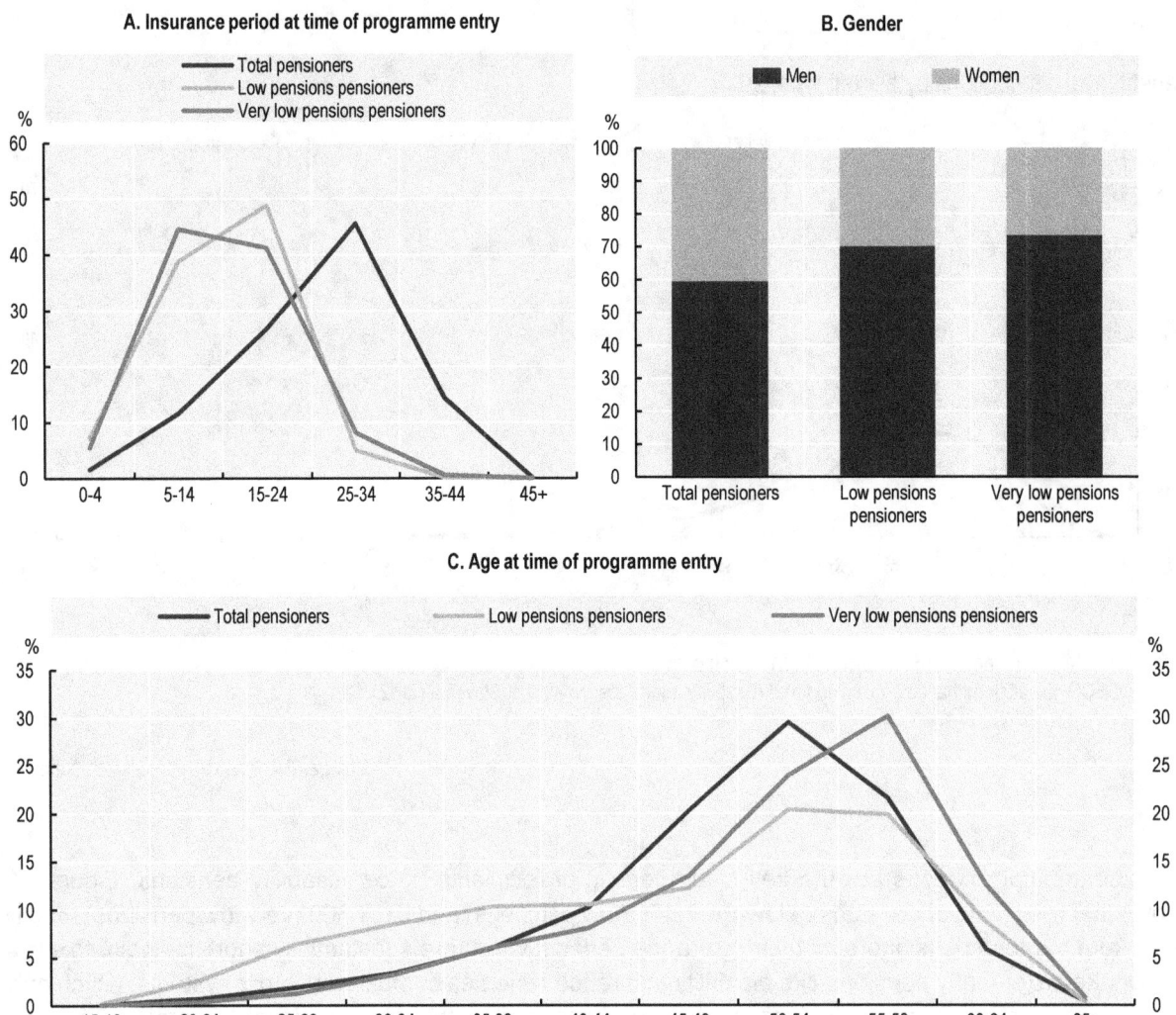

Note: Low pensions pensioners are defined as these receiving less than the Basic Minimum Income (EUR 402.18 per month), while very low pensions pensioners receive less than EUR 300 per month.
Source: OECD calculations based on Pension and Disability Insurance Institute of Slovenia (ZPIZ) data www.zpiz.si/.

StatLink ⟶ https://stat.link/2kg4bp

Partial disability payments follow a distribution similar to disability pensions, but with lesser variation. The distribution of partial disability payments follows an inverted-U shape, like that of disability pensions. Naturally, its maximum is around half that of disability pensions, but it has a lower standard deviation, indicating that payments are more concentrated around a given amount (EUR 200-EUR 400 per month). The long tail of higher pension payments observed among full pensioners is not present among partial disability beneficiaries. One potential explanation could be that women in Slovenia, who are most often the beneficiaries of partial disability, have more concentrated labour earnings, across all levels of income (SURS, 2020[7]). This would result in more concentrated disability payments.

Table 3.6. The average period of disability insurance benefit receipt is long, making its low benefit payments highly inadequate

Average spell duration on disability pension and disability insurance benefits by gender, 2019

|  | Men | | Women | |
| --- | --- | --- | --- | --- |
|  | Years | Months | Years | Months |
| Disability pension | 21 | 3 | 27 | 1 |
| Disability insurance benefit | 6 | 0 | 5 | 2 |

Source: OECD calculations based on Pension and Disability Insurance Institute of Slovenia (ZPIZ) data, www.zpiz.si/.

StatLink https://stat.link/tmri1q

There is no evidence on the outflow from ZPIZ beneficiaries and the destination of people leaving the system, which in itself speaks to the capacity of ZPIZ to evaluate its programmes and policies. Table 3.6 suggests that the exit rate from disability insurance and disability pension is very low. Another way to approximate a figure on the exit rate from disability insurance is to rely on ESS records, which can provide information on the trajectories of partial ZPIZ beneficiaries. It is important to note that the outflows to employment observed among partial ZPIZ beneficiaries is not a good proxy for the entire universe of disability pension and benefit recipients. First, because partial ZPIZ beneficiaries are less severely disabled (although they could be comparable to disability beneficiaries, see Table 3.5). Second, the outflow to employment may be larger for partial ZPIZ beneficiaries, as they are activated by the ESS. Recipients of a disability pension or benefit, on the contrary, are not activated at all. With these caveats in mind, Table 3.7 summarises the outflow to employment from partial disability beneficiaries registered at ESS.

Table 3.7. Outflow rates to employment are larger for claimants with better labour market options

Outflow to employment as a share of claimants for partial ZPIZ beneficiaries by characteristics, 2017-20

| Total | Share | Sex | Share | Education | Share | Age | Share |
| --- | --- | --- | --- | --- | --- | --- | --- |
| Total | 9% | Men | 10% | Primary school and less | 6% | 25-29 | 28% |
|  |  | Women | 9% | Vocational education | 9% | 30-34 | 23% |
|  |  |  |  | Secondary education | 15% | 35-39 | 23% |
|  |  |  |  | Tertiary education | 17% | 40-44 | 16% |
|  |  |  |  |  |  | 45-49 | 13% |
|  |  |  |  |  |  | 50-54 | 10% |
|  |  |  |  |  |  | 55-59 | 7% |
|  |  |  |  |  |  | 60+ | 3% |

ZPIZ: Pension and Disability Insurance Institute of Slovenia. ESS: Employment Service of Slovenia.
Note: Share of outflows to employment are calculated as the fraction of transitions of ZPIZ recipients registered at ESS from unemployment register to employment in a given year over stock of ZPIZ recipients registered at ESS, for a given group of characteristics.
Source: OECD calculations based on European Social Survey data, https://www.europeansocialsurvey.org/data/.

StatLink https://stat.link/wgoz7y

Outflow rates to employment are larger for claimants with better labour market possibilities and more adaptability. On average over the period 2017-20, the outflow from unemployment to employment for partial disability beneficiaries was 9%. Outflow increases with educational attainment, in line with better labour market opportunities for higher-skilled workers. Outflow to employment decreases with age, as younger claimants are more adaptable to change jobs that suit their residual employment capacity. The systems of disability and unemployment insurance, both relatively more generous for older workers, may also be partly discourage the transition to work of older workers.

## 3.4. Occupational injuries and diseases

Slovenia's sickness and disability system has one other anomaly, as there are only minor differences between occupational and general injuries and diseases. Slovenia regulates general and occupational injuries and diseases in the same sickness and disability insurance systems, albeit with some differences in the access to and level of benefit payments. For instance, there is no minimum work period required in case of work-caused accidents or diseases, and benefit payments are higher. In most other EU and OECD countries, special workers' compensation schemes are in place for work accidents and occupational diseases, often with rules very different from those applying to the general sickness and disability system and with a strong focus on returning work-injured workers to work as quickly as possible.

The uniform approach in Slovenia has two undesirable consequences, the first being that the costs of work accidents are largely socialised. Workers' compensation schemes in most EU and OECD countries use sector-specific premiums in line with the accident risk in a particular sector or, in just a few countries, even a particular company. The per-person premium in a sector with a high accident risk can sometimes be 20 or even 30 times higher than in another sector with a low risk. The main idea being that higher employer costs promote investments in working conditions and the prevention of work-caused sickness and disability. This is not currently the case in Slovenia, where all employers pay the same contributions to sickness and disability insurance. The 30-day sick-pay obligation for each sickness case provides a certain incentive for Slovenian employers to prevent accidents and occupational diseases.

A second problem of the uniform approach is that occupational diseases are virtually non-existent. The legislation in Slovenia does not acknowledge that work can cause illness, leaving a share of workers less well protected than they should be. The outdated list of occupational diseases does not reflect the current strain of the workplace and, every year, only a handful of people are assessed as having experienced an occupational disease. Accordingly, mental health conditions for example will never qualify as occupationally caused even though many of those people will have a harder time navigating the system.

## 3.5. Co-operation between ZPIZ and ZZZS

Despite the natural linkages and overlaps between sickness and disability insurance programmes, information sharing across responsible institutions is uncommon. Sickness insurance is the gateway to disability insurance for employed persons: workers on sickness insurance whose health issue cannot be improved through medical treatment should, in theory, transition to disability insurance. This feature clearly requires a certain co-ordination between the ZZZS and the ZPIZ, which should co-ordinate on their assessment decisions, or at least, share information on claimants. At present, this is not the case. Rather than working on a single register that automatically collects the relevant information, both institutions need to collect data on the applicant, which in many instances is duplicated as the information requirements for both programmes are similar. This slows down the process and generates unnecessary administrative costs. This also requires additional information validation processes, conducted by both the ZZZS and the ZPIZ, which would be redundant should both institutions share information.

The lack of uniformity in ZZZS and ZPIZ assessments is especially problematic in Slovenia, as sickness and disability insurance cover similar risks. As shown in the first section of this report, sickness insurance is frequently used for long-term sickness, a role that should arguably be taken over by disability insurance. With such a blurry definition of the risks covered by the two types of insurance, the lack of uniformity in assessments is particular problematic. Two main elements create a dichotomy in the assessment of sickness and disability:

- Disability assessment has an occupational component, while sickness assessment is exclusively medically based;
- Sickness insurance requires claimants to be undergoing a medical treatment, while eligibility for disability benefits hinges on a complete medical treatment.

As a result of the first difference, a worker may not be eligible for disability insurance if the health ailment is not work limiting, but could be entitled to sickness insurance for years. The second difference opens substantial room for interpretation, particularly for mental health conditions. Both elements imply that many people in Slovenia may stay on sickness benefits, possibly even for years, without applying for, or being entitled to, disability insurance rights. Without co-ordination of the assessment across the two institutes, but also within, the social protection system for persons with disability is too lenient for some, but has significant coverage gaps for others.

Another reason for frequent long-term sickness absences is that people may not transition to the disability programme even with permanent disabilities. This is mainly due to the relative generosity of the sickness programme compared to disability insurance, further accentuated by the lack of co-ordination between the ZZZS and the ZPIZ. The institutions do not share sufficient information to ensure a timely transition from sickness insurance to disability insurance, and the decision relies too much on the own claimant's responsibility, who does not have financial incentives to request such a transition.

A single medical expert body for the assessment of sickness and disability could help to uniform the assessment and reduce the administrative burden. The 2010 Working Group, formed by ZZZS and ZPIZ experts, first presented the idea of a new body, the New Medical Expert Organisation. The same idea reappears in the 2016 White Paper on Pensions. The goal of streamlining the assessment of both institutions is to increase professionalism, unify criteria, and ensure the independence of the assessors. If properly implemented, a single body could enable co-ordination across the two institutes but also uniform assessment within institutes, across local offices and assessors. It would also enable modernising the IT systems for recording data of applicants to both programmes, shortening waiting times after application.

Coordination between the ZZZS and the ZPIZ must get support from the top. Currently, any efforts to co-ordinate across the two institutes comes from the bottom. Assessors, GPs and assessment committees are aware of the lack of co-ordination and its consequences, and make efforts to reach out across institutes. This is clearly insufficient, and even the creation of a joint assessment committee may not solve all issues. The Ministry of Health and the MoLFSA also have to improve their co-ordination, at all levels. One example of failed co-ordination is in defining the budget allocated to the sickness and disability institutes.

## References

Autor, D., M. Duggan and J. Gruber (2014), "Moral Hazard and Claims Deterrence in Private Disability Insurance", *American Economic Journal: Applied Economics*, Vol. 6/4, pp. 110-141, http://dx.doi.org/10.1257/app.6.4.110. [3]

Comission, B. (ed.) (2019), *ESPN Thematic Report on Financing social protection - Slovenia*, European Social Policy Network (ESPN). [1]

Fialho, P. and J. Høj (2020), "Labour market institutions for an ageing labour force in Slovenia", *OECD Economics Department Working Papers*, No. 1648, OECD Publishing, Paris, https://dx.doi.org/10.1787/9eca1535-en. [5]

MacDonald, D., C. Prinz and H. Immervoll (2020), "Can disability benefits promote (re)employment? : Considerations for effective disability benefit design", *OECD Social, Employment and Migration Working Papers*, No. 253, OECD Publishing, Paris, https://dx.doi.org/10.1787/227e7990-en. [8]

MISSOC (2021), *MISSOC Comparative tables*, https://www.missoc.org/missoc-database/comparative-tables/results/ (accessed on 4 November 2021). [2]

OECD (2015), *Fit Mind, Fit Job: From Evidence to Practice in Mental Health and Work*, Mental Health and Work, OECD Publishing, Paris, https://dx.doi.org/10.1787/9789264228283-en. [6]

OECD (2010), *Sickness, Disability and Work: Breaking the Barriers: A Synthesis of Findings across OECD Countries*, OECD Publishing, Paris, https://dx.doi.org/10.1787/9789264088856-en. [4]

SURS (2020), *stat.si*, https://www.stat.si/StatWeb/en/News/Index/9073. [7]

## Notes

[1] Slovenia therefore belongs to the group of countries with a pension-type disability insurance, contrary to countries with either a dedicated unemployment-type disability insurance or a flat-rate disability benefit (MacDonald, Prinz and Immervoll, 2020[8]). The setup implies that any deficit of the disability insurance is invisible under the broader pension programme.

[2] Upon reaching the retirement age, people could choose to switch to an old-age pension if conditions for entitlement to the latter would be satisfied, but with no impact on the level of payment that they receive.

# 4 The role of unemployment benefits, employment services and social assistance for jobseekers with health limitations in Slovenia

Slovenia's unemployment insurance and the public employment service play an important role for people with health problems or disabilities, in various ways. First, people who are unemployed do not qualify for sickness insurance and remain in the unemployment insurance. Second, people with partial disability benefits must register with the employment service. Third, people with insufficient employment records do not qualify for insurance benefits and have to rely on social assistance and the employment service. This setup implies that many of those with most severe health issues and labour market barriers are under the responsibility of the unemployment system. Accordingly, the public employment service has strong services in place, including employment rehabilitation and systematic assessment of health barriers to employment. However, systematic support is provided only after many years although new analysis presented in this report shows that an early provision of active labour market programmes is essential for a successful transition to employment. Problems can only be solved by co-ordinated sickness, disability and unemployment insurance reform.

The Slovenian sickness and disability insurance system creates a dichotomy in two ways: first, between persons falling ill while employed and unemployed (as the latter are not entitled to sickness benefits); and second, between persons with disability by years of contributions paid into the disability insurance system (excluding those with a limited work record). As a result, unemployment benefits and social assistance are the sole benefit programmes available for many persons with disability and long-term sickness, giving a key role to the Public Employment Services. This section describes the approaches to profile health barriers to employment among jobseekers, and the main characteristics of unemployment and social assistance.

## 4.1. Profiling health limitations among unemployed workers

### 4.1.1. Registration at the Employment Service of Slovenia

The first step to profiling unemployed workers is registration to the ESS, which is only mandatory for the unemployed with unemployment insurance or disability benefit entitlement. Because the ESS administers unemployment benefits, there is an obligation for these unemployed to register at the ESS within 30 days from the termination of their employment contract. Disability benefit recipients (partial and full) who are without a job are also required to register at the ESS. Instead, jobseekers not eligible for contributory social support are not obliged to register. Some countries, like Germany or Switzerland, oblige discouraged workers to register with the PES, allowing to activate them earlier (OECD, 2016[1]).

Despite the incentives put in place, about one in four unemployed do not register with the ESS, possibly concentrating a large proportion of persons with severe health limitations. The ESS has a number of programmes in place for unemployed persons, in particular for those unemployed facing social exclusion or health barriers to employment, which could incentivise their registration. For example, the ESS collaborates with the Centres of Social Work (*Centri za socialno delo*), responsible for administering social assistance, to help jobseekers not entitled to social insurance benefits find some form of social support. ESS caseworkers also help jobseekers with disability obtain a legal disability status, in addition to the services available through the Employment Rehabilitation and Employment of Disabled Persons Act (ZZRZI), described here and in later sections. Despite these forms of support, it is estimated that one in four unemployed persons, particularly those with low labour market attachment and socially excluded, do not register with the ESS (OECD, 2016[1]).

### 4.1.2. Engaging unemployed workers with health barriers

ESS clients facing health barriers to employment fall under one of three main groups, depending on whether they have a recognised disability status. Precisely, the three categories include (1) holders of a legal status of disability; (2) unemployed recipients of partial disability benefits or pension from ZPIZ; and (3) jobseekers with disclosed or suspected health issues. Clients from the first two groups have a recognised disability, while clients from the last group do not.

The ESS plays a key role in identifying the clients with potentially limiting barriers to employment and providing them with a recognised disability status. Persons with a legal disability status and recipients of ZPIZ benefits automatically fall into the group of jobseekers with barriers to employment due to health issues. Other jobseekers with disclosed or suspected health issues represent a greater challenge, as they need to be identified and profiled, and in most cases, require raising their own understanding on their health limitations. The ESS plays a key role in this process, by profiling these clients according to their employability (see Box 4.1), and granting them a status of disability under the ZZRZI act. Such recognition of disability is key to preventing these people from continuously falling between the cracks of the safety net for persons with disability. Data suggest that in 80% of the cases, the work of the ESS results in the acquisition of a disability status. The remaining 20% result in employment rehabilitation without granting a disability status (more on employment rehabilitation in Chapter 2).

The ESS takes a systematic approach to identifying health issues as a barrier to employment, specified by the ZZRZI act. First, jobseekers with potential health barriers to employment have regular meetings with their caseworkers in their regional ESS office. In case a disclosed or suspected health issue, there is an attempt to contact the personal GP to get his or her opinion on the extent to which the client's health issues are a limitation to work. If this is not possible, caseworkers can refer jobseekers to a medical assessment, which provides a first opinion on the potential work barriers. This may result in a referral to additional assessments, as these defined under the ZZRZI. At the beginning of the process, jobseekers receive an assessment of their health, skills and functional capacities under the so-called Service B. Then the regional rehabilitation commission, together with the ESS caseworker, decides on the individual programme for each jobseeker with health limitations. Only in the last step, jobseekers will receive formal support to find suitable employment.

Identification of health barriers is coming long after registration with the ESS. Table 4.1 shows that only 14% of the jobseekers undergo the initial medical assessment in the first five months from their first registration with the ESS. The large majority (56%) undergo the initial medical assessment two years or more after initial registration. This is a result of the difficulty of identifying jobseekers with health barriers to employment. It also shows that, despite the well-structured approach of the ESS, jobseekers with health barriers spend long periods before receiving targeted support, possibly leading to a further deterioration of their labour market position.

Table 4.1. Identifying health barriers to employment takes a long time at the ESS

Share of ESS registered jobseekers undergoing medical treatment by months spent since initial registration, 2019

|  | Number of recipients undergoing medical assessment | Share |
| --- | --- | --- |
| 0-5 months | 420 | 14% |
| 6-11 months | 355 | 12% |
| 12-23 months | 560 | 19% |
| 24+ months | 1 680 | 56% |

ESS: Employment Service of Slovenia.
Note: Includes all registered jobseekers, including recipients of social assistance and recipients of disability benefits or pension.
Source: European Social Survey data, www.europeansocialsurvey.org/data/.

StatLink https://stat.link/5il76g

The ESS deals with high caseloads for its counsellors and long waiting times at rehabilitation providers. On average, there are around 300 cases per counsellor. For those specialised in rehabilitation counselling, the number of cases can go up to 400, but with substantial geographical variation (Table 4.2). These factors compound the difficulty of identifying and profiling jobseekers with health limitations, who usually experience very severe health barriers to work, often from mental health causes, with a great share of socially excluded cases. The high caseload prevents providing the regular support needed to motivate jobseekers with complex barriers. Added to this, waiting times for rehabilitation services can be very long, with a one-year waiting time being the norm rather than the exception.

Table 4.2. High caseloads for counsellors and long waiting times at rehabilitation providers further complicate the work of the ESS

Average cases per caseworker in regional ESS offices and standard deviation for selected offices

|  | Average cases per caseworker | Standard deviation (selected regional offices) |
| --- | --- | --- |
| Celje | 361 | |
| Koper | 342 | |
| Kranj | 416 | |
| Ljubjana | 360 | 157 |
| Maribor | 376 | 155 |
| Murska Sobota | 362 | |
| Nova Gorica | 360 | 112 |
| Novo Mesto | 296 | |
| Ptuj | 285 | |
| Sevnica | 314 | |
| Trbovlje | 306 | |
| Velenje | 329 | |

ESS: Employment Service of Slovenia.
Note: Cases per caseworker are calculated as the number of registered jobseekers over the number of caseworkers in a given office. Standard deviation is reported only for those regional offices with high case variability, potentially explained by a variable number of jobseekers.
Source: European Social Survey data, www.europeansocialsurvey.org/data/.

StatLink https://stat.link/rhxw4u

The collaboration of the ESS and the Centres for Social Work is key to improve the help given to jobseekers with severe health barriers to employment. Centres for Social Work (CSW) are responsible for paying social assistance and providing support to individuals and families in difficult personal or social circumstances. CSW are under responsibility of the municipalities, with each Centre reporting directly to the ministry. There is a formalised co-operation channel between the ESS and CSW since 2012 for social assistance claimants and other registered unemployed with complex barriers to employment (e.g. mental health problems, addiction, and social problems). A joint ESS and CSW commission is responsible for the assessment of provisional non-employability of such clients (see Box 4.1. The Commission's task is to establish labour market barriers, decide which of the institutions is responsible for the client, and make suggestions for intervention (OECD, 2016[1]).

### 4.1.3. Descriptive statistics: jobseekers with health barriers to employment or disability

Measuring the incidence of disability is difficult, just as it is difficult for ESS caseworkers to identify health barriers to employment. There are several approaches possible, some of which are applicable beyond research purposes to actual profiling of health barriers to employment:

- One approach is to rely on official statuses of disability, which is the approach of the ESS. This could include ZPIZ beneficiaries, holders of a legal disability status, or disabilities recognised under the ZZRZI act. This method possibly results in an underestimation of the actual health barriers to employment, as many jobseekers experiencing them do not have a recognised disability status.
- Another approach to measure the health barriers to employment is to rely on the ESS caseworkers' assessment to halt job search obligations due to health reasons. When these breaks are long, they could be the consequence of a disability or significant health barrier to employment.

- A last approach, at present useful for research purposes, is to rely on survey data available. Using EU-SILC data, for example, one can identify persons with disability using the health and disability questions of the survey. European or national population surveys could complement administrative data to help public employment services calibrate their statistical profiling models.

Data suggest that about one in six registered unemployed have a recognised disability, but there is substantial regional variation. The ESS estimates that 17% of the registered unemployed have a recognised disability. This figure, however, masks substantial variation across regions, ranging from 10% (in Kranj) to 29% (in Murska Sobota). Figure 4.1 exemplifies this regional variation.

Figure 4.1. There is substantial regional variation in the rate of unemployed persons with disability

Share of unemployed persons with disability out of total unemployed by ESS regional units, 2019

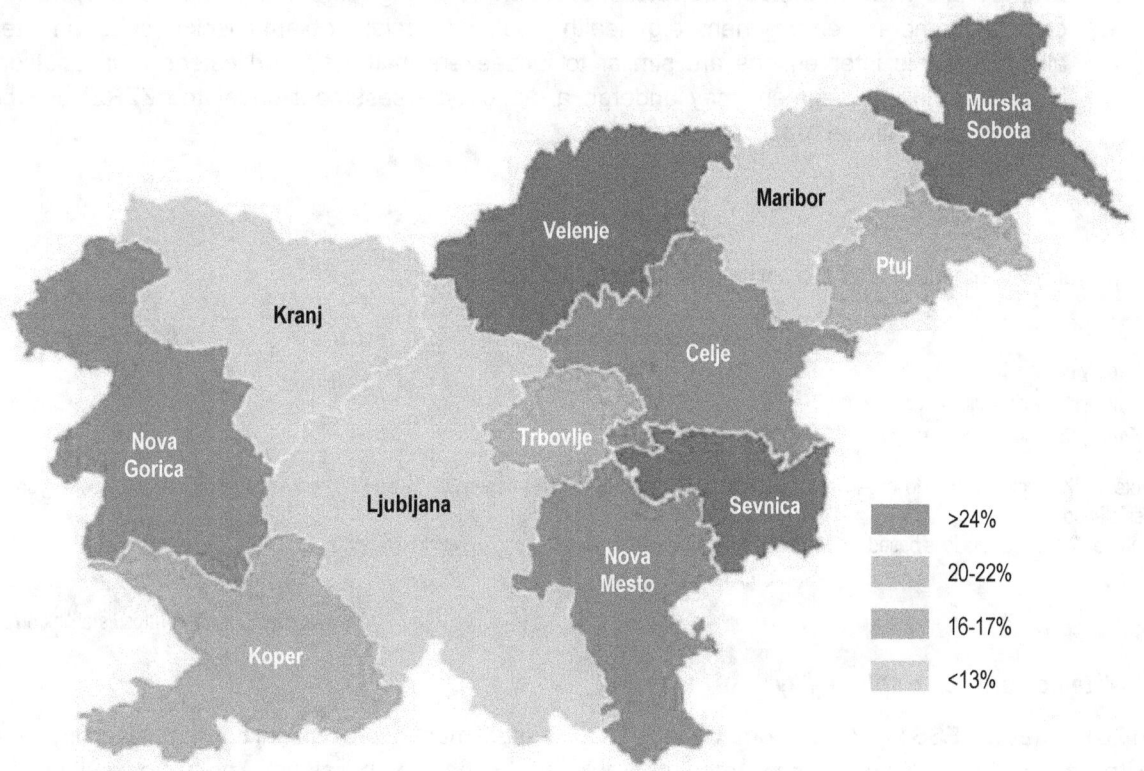

ESS: Employment Service of Slovenia.
Source: OECD calculations based on European Social Survey, www.europeansocialsurvey.org/data/ and the Statistical Office of the Republic of Slovenia (SURS) www.stat.si/statweb/en.

### Box 4.1. Profiling the employability of ESS and Centres for Social Work (CSW)

**ESS employability segments**

ESS counsellors assign clients to one of three client segments:

- **Directly employable**: Motivated jobseekers with relevant skills and no particular barriers to employment.
- **Employable with additional activities**: Jobseekers requiring additional support from a counsellor to maintain motivation, acquire new skills, or overcome health or other barriers. Jobseekers may receive in-depth career counselling, participate in group-sessions and be referred to shorter workshops or suitable labour market programmes.
- **Employable with intensive support**: Jobseekers requiring more intensive help to overcome complex barriers to employment (e.g. health problems, social problems, lack of skills, an often all of it). Basic interventions are similar to jobseekers in the second category. In addition, jobseekers in this segment may undergo a disability assessment under the ZZRZI and be referred to vocational rehabilitation services.

Table 4.3. Partial ZPIZ recipients are most often employable with intensive support

Employability segment by type of main income support, 2017-20

|  | All registered jobseekers | ZPIZ recipients | FSA recipients |
|---|---|---|---|
| Directly employable | 19% | 0% | 10% |
| Employable with additional activities | 45% | 20% | 47% |
| Employable with intensive support | 36% | 80% | 43% |

Note: ZPIZ recipients refers to jobseekers receiving partial disability benefits or pension, while FSA recipients refers to those receiving social assistance.
Source: OECD calculations based on European Social Survey, www.europeansocialsurvey.org/data/.

StatLink https://stat.link/5i7bvj

*CSW temporary non-employability*

In 2012, the joint ESS and CSW Commissions for the assessment of provisional non-employability were established. The ESS refers registered unemployed to the Commissions. The Commissions are organised on the local level and consist of at least three members (employment adviser, social worker and rehabilitation adviser plus additional experts depending on the individual's specific problems), which are jointly appointed by the manager of the local ESS and the manager of the responsible CSW. However, often the ESS and CSW advisers participating in the Commission have not dealt with the respective client before. The discussion of the Commission can result in two possible outcomes:

- **Temporary non-employability**: The local CSW is then the primary responsible institution. The person may be entitled to social assistance, upon entering into an agreement on resolving social problems, but cannot continue claiming unemployment insurance.
- **Continued unemployment status**: The individual remains in the ESS unemployment register, but is assigned to the local CSW to follow a personalised action plan for social inclusion.

Source: OECD (2016[1]), *Connecting People with Jobs The Labour Market, Activation Policies and Disadvantaged Workers in Slovenia*, https://doi.org/10.1787/9789264265349-en.

Women and jobseekers with lower educational attainment are exempt from job search due to health reasons more often. Figure 4.2 shows the share of jobseekers exempted of job search obligations due to health reasons by sex and educational attainment. Women are consistently more often than men exempted from job search. One explanation might be that job search exemptions include caring for a family member, a role more often taken up by women. This higher incidence of exemptions among women also holds for durations longer than three months, which makes it less likely that care to a family member is the main cause of the gender differences observed. Across both genders, the figure shows a negative relationship between the incidence of job-search exemptions and educational attainment. This is not surprising, and it is in line with a wide literature documenting the correlations between education and health (Cutler, Lleras-Muney and Vogl, 2008[2]).

Linking ESS employability status and job-search exemptions due to health reasons suggests that over one-third of those employable with in-depth support are exempt from job search. This approach shows that the employability classification of the ESS provides an (imperfect) proxy of measuring health barriers to employment.

Data from population surveys suggest that over 30% of unemployed persons in Slovenia have a disability. This figure, which is naturally higher than the figure obtained using recognised disabilities and job-search exemptions, shows that there is probably a significant share of jobseekers with health barriers to employment whose disability is not recognised in any way.

Figure 4.2. Women and jobseekers with low educational attainment are exempt from job search due to health reasons more often

Share of jobseekers exempt from job search due to health reasons, by educational attainment and sex, 2019

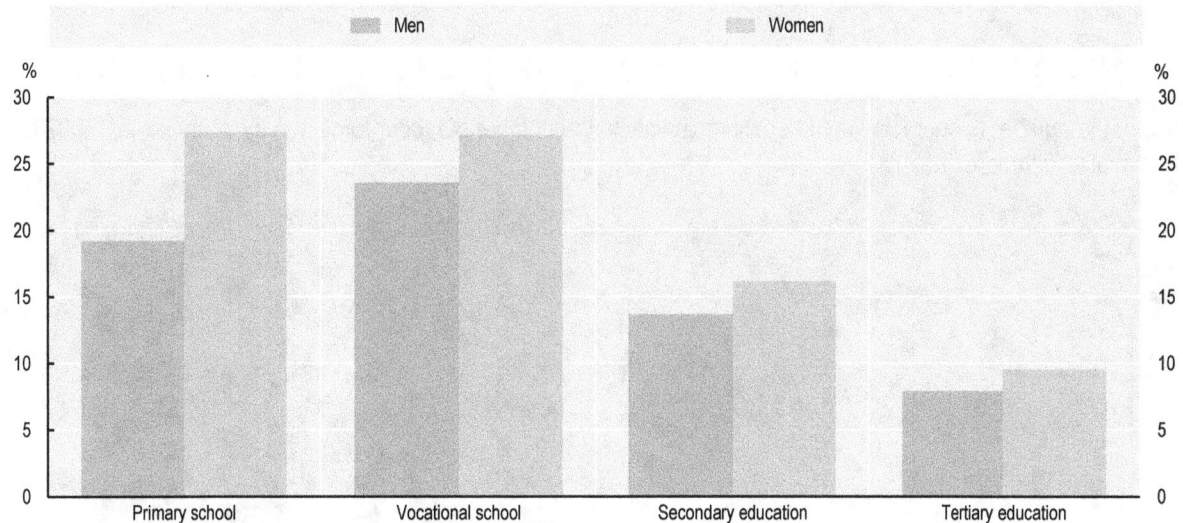

Note: Jobseekers exempted from job search due to health reasons are limited to these exemptions of 30 days or longer. Causes for exemption include being unable to work due to health reasons and caring for a family member.
Source: OECD calculations based on European Social Survey, www.europeansocialsurvey.org/data/.

StatLink https://stat.link/7gx8zv

Table 4.4. Over one-third of those employable with in-depth support are exempt from job search

Jobseekers exempted from job search due to health reason by employability, 2019

|  | Jobseekers exempted from job search | Share over employability category |
| --- | --- | --- |
| Directly employable | 450 | 4% |
| Employable with additional activities | 3 269 | 10% |
| Employable with in depth support | 10 627 | 35% |

Note: Shares are calculated by taking the jobseekers exempted from job search in 2019 over the number of jobseekers classified in the corresponding employability category.
Source: OECD calculations based on European Social Survey, www.europeansocialsurvey.org/data/.

StatLink ᐧᒥᔕᒥ https://stat.link/5g9e4a

## 4.2. Social protection for jobseekers with disability

### 4.2.1. Unemployment insurance

Unemployment insurance (UI) is a right acquired for employees, self-employed and recipients of sickness benefits, who have lost their job involuntarily. Benefits are available for insured persons having contributed for at least nine months during the previous 24 months. For the unemployed under 30, only six months of contributions are required. Involuntary unemployment includes no-fault layoffs from permanent and after fixed-term contracts. Despite this being a strict condition, only applied in about a third of OECD countries, it is de facto not a binding one. Evidence shows that there is significant collusion with employers to overcome this condition (OECD, 2016[1]).

Figure 4.3. Few unemployed receive unemployment benefits compared to international standards

Ratio of the number of unemployment benefit recipients to the number of labour force survey unemployed, 2007 or latest available year

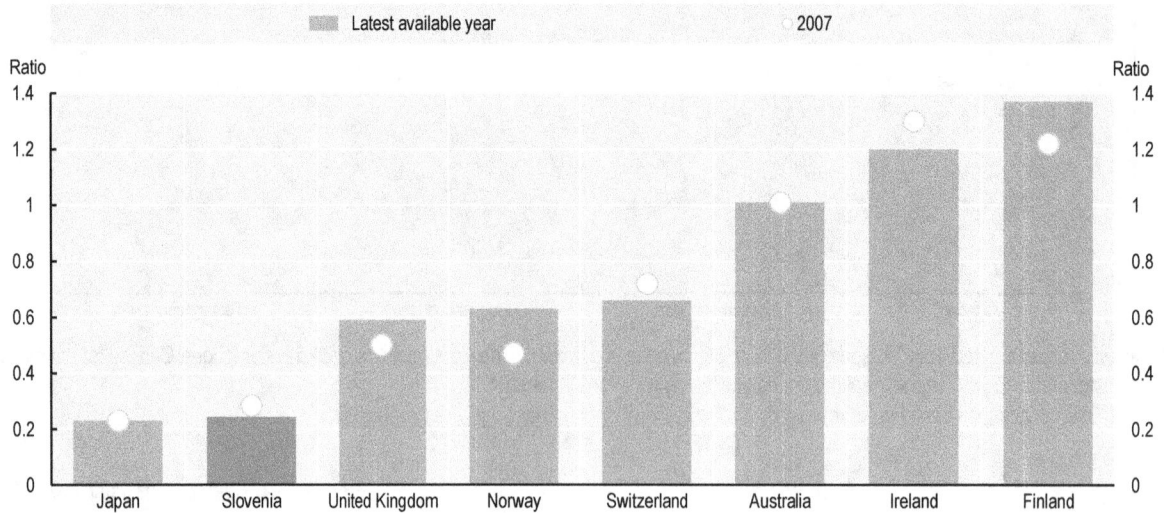

Source: OECD (2016), *Connecting People with Jobs: The Labour Market, Activation Policies and Disadvantaged Workers in Slovenia*, Connecting People with Jobs, OECD Publishing, Paris, https://doi.org/10.1787/9789264265349-en and OECD compilation based on labour force survey data.

StatLink ᐧᒥᔕᒥ https://stat.link/rtxk2e

In Slovenia, the benefit duration for receipt of unemployment benefit strongly increases with work experience and age. The maximum benefit duration varies from two months for young workers with 6-8 months of prior employment to 25 months for most workers over age 55. The system creates strong disincentives for older workers to work, especially those over age 57 (entitled to unemployment benefit for 25 months with nine months of employment in the past 24 months). These parameters mean that seasonal employment can be sufficient for older workers to re-establish UI eligibility and thus weaken their incentives to seek permanent employment (OECD, 2016[1]). While longer UI entitlement for older workers is common among OECD countries, Slovenia's system is especially generous for older workers.

The replacement rate is high for short unemployment spells, and decreases significantly for longer spell durations. The replacement rate is 80%, 60% and 50% for months 1-3, 4-12, and 13 or more, respectively, of benefit receipt. The benefit depends on the average monthly earnings in the past nine months (five months for younger workers), subject to a minimum gross monthly payment of EUR 350 and a maximum of EUR 892.50 (the latter was decreased from EUR 1 050 in May 2012) (OECD, 2016[1]). The replacement rate was also increased during this reform, reducing the incentives to transition from unemployment to employment (Vodopivec et al., 2015[3]).

In Slovenia, relatively few unemployed receive unemployment benefits compared to international standards. Countries like Switzerland or the Netherlands, which have comparable unemployment benefit systems to Slovenia in that they offer a single contributory unemployment insurance programme, have a share of unemployment receipt among the unemployed that is twice as high (Figure 4.4). The low take up rate in Slovenia has a number of explanations, including the condition of involuntary unemployment, the lower unemployment duration, the relative strictness of unemployment benefit eligibility and generosity for workers under age 50, and rather strict requirements to register with the ESS.

Figure 4.4. In Slovenia, relatively few unemployed receive unemployment benefits

Composition of registered unemployed persons by source of income and age, 2019

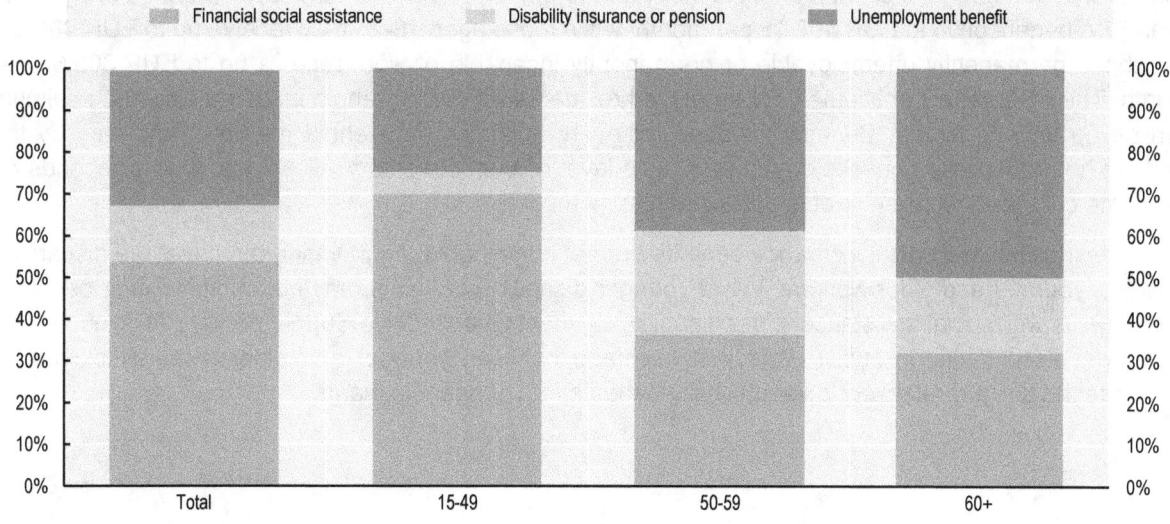

Source: OECD calculations based on European Social Survey, www.europeansocialsurvey.org/data/.

StatLink https://stat.link/r98bfj

Take-up of unemployment benefit take is relatively low for workers under age 50. Benefit eligibility and duration of payments are relatively stricter for workers younger than 50, which represent over 65% of the registered unemployed. Figure 4.4 shows that jobseekers under age 50 rely heavily on social assistance as the main source of income, as the result of a lower eligibility for social insurance. As jobseekers become older, the reliance on social assistance diminishes and entitlement to unemployment benefits increases. Above age 50, disability benefits are also important as a source of income. Overall, more than half of all registered jobseekers relies on social assistance and one-third receive unemployment benefits.

### 4.2.2. Social assistance

All residents in Slovenia are entitled to social support to guarantee a Basic Minimum Income *(osnovni znesek minimalnega dohodka)*. There are three means-tested social assistance programmes:

- Financial social assistance (FSA) providing temporary social support to those in need (up to three months initially, extendable to six months, and up to 12 months for older workers);
- Emergency social assistance (EFSA) granted to residents living in a situation of temporary material deprivation due to exceptional living costs that they cannot meet with their own income;
- Supplementary Allowance granted (also permanently) to older residents, age 63/65 or older for women/men, persons with a permanent incapacity to work, or those permanently unemployed.

All benefits are organised centrally, but managed at the regional level, by local Centres for Social Work.

Social assistance entitlement in Slovenia has a strong activation component, which is important given that it is the main benefit for most jobseekers. Eligibility to social assistance requires all working age recipients to register with the ESS, participate in ALMPs, and actively search employment. Failure to satisfy these conditions results in a loss of social assistance payments. Those with severe health issues or work incapacity, however, are exempt from these conditions.

The level of benefits depends on number of household members, their age and number of working hours. Table 4.5 summarises the benefit level by status of the recipient. Unemployed workers are entitled to an FSA benefit of up to EUR 402.18 per month, while those aged 18-26 may receive up to EUR 281.53, and those permanently unemployable or permanently incapable of work receive up to EUR 305.66 per month. The FSA benefit entitlement for employed residents with a household income below the minimum can be up to 50% higher. Benefits increase for every additional household member, and vary by the working hours of these household members. The level of Supplementary Allowance, which depends on the same criteria, is worth 47% of the Basic Minimum Income.

Social assistance and social insurance benefits are not combinable, aggravating the coverage disparities between younger and older workers. While younger disability claimants may not combine their pensions and benefits with social assistance, older disability claimants may receive Supplementary Allowance. This creates a discontinuity in social protection coverage between younger and older disability claimants, adding to the already relatively lower disability benefits for younger claimants.

Table 4.5. The level of social assistance benefits depends on household composition, age and the number of hours worked

Basic Minimum Income for the calculation of the FSA by household status, 2019

|  | Base | EUR per month |
|---|---|---|
| Single adult | 1.00 | 402.18 |
| Single adult working 60-128 hours per month (activity allowance) | 1.26 | 506.75 |
| Single adult working more than 128 hours per month (activity allowance) | 1.51 | 607.29 |
| Single person aged 18-26, registered at the ESS | 0.70 | 281.53 |
| Single adult permanently unemployed, permanently incapable of working, or older than 63 (65 for men) | 0.76 | 305.66 |
| Additional benefit for every additional adult in the household | 0.57 | 229.24 |
| Additional benefit for every additional employed adult working more than 128 hours per month | 0.83 | 333.81 |
| Additional benefit for every additional employed adult working 60 to 128 hours per month | 0.70 | 281.53 |
| Child of a person claiming social assistance | 0.59 | 237.29 |
| Additional benefit for every child in a single parent family | 0.18 | 72.39 |

FSA: Financial Social Assistance.
Note: FSA benefits correspond to the difference between the Basic Minimum Income and the household income.
Source: GOV.si.

StatLink https://stat.link/kte6g5

Contrary to social insurance, social assistance's rights accrue at the household level, creating potential coverage gaps. Social assistance plays a key role in Slovenia, and replaces social insurance for a large number of unemployed and under-employed workers. Eligibility for social assistance is, which like in most countries is means-tested at the household level, requires the household income (including income from social insurance) to fall below basic minimum income, and property and assets to be under EUR 19 304. Homeowners with very low income may not be eligible. Young persons with disability, with insufficient years of contributions for entitlement to ZPIZ benefits, may not receive any form of support if they still live in a household that does not meet the conditions for FSA eligibility. This results in a lack of income support but also removes any incentive to register at the ESS, furthering their social exclusion. High reliance on social assistance to prevent social exclusion goes hand-in-hand with large coverage gaps.

### 4.2.3. Partial ZPIZ benefit or pensions

ZPIZ benefits represent a non-negligible source of income for many unemployed workers, particularly those over age 50 with sufficient contributory periods. Figure 4.4 above shows that 13% of jobseekers receive a partial disability benefit or pension, a share peaking at 25% for the age group 50 to 59 and falling to 18% for those over age 60. There is strong positive correlation between contributory years and receipt of ZPIZ benefits. Two elements seem to be in play: (1) older workers tend to experience more disabilities, and (2) the system encourages older workers with more contributions to take up ZPIZ benefits. While (1) is universally true,[1] the fact that ZPIZ take up does not linearly increase with age suggests that (2) plays a major role. The system requires a minimum level of contributions for eligibility, which is binding particularly at younger ages. It also creates a discontinuity at age 50, by which those over 50 face a more generous benefit system.

This duality of social protection for persons with disability in Slovenia can partly explain why ESS jobseekers with health limitations have employability lower than for ZPIZ recipients. Only persons with disability with relatively long employment histories (or years of contributions) are eligible for ZPIZ benefits.

Persons with disability with shorter contribution periods, possibly due to more severe health limitations and greater detachment from the labour market, are among the pool of jobseekers not eligible for ZPIZ benefits. Table 4.1 illustrates this idea, by showing that the rate of temporarily non-employable is higher among social assistance recipients than among ZPIZ beneficiaries. This is a common feature in countries with a pension-like disability insurance. In countries with other systems, those with severe disability are the most likely to receive benefits from disability insurance while in Slovenia, many of them will be under the responsibility of the ESS or the local welfare offices.

Table 4.6. ESS jobseekers with health limitations have employability lower than for ZPIZ recipients

Number of registered jobseekers temporarily non-employable and share over registered jobseekers by main type of income support, 2019

|  | Temporarily non-employable | Share of non-employable over registered jobseekers |
| --- | --- | --- |
| FSA payment | 5 789 | 18% |
| ZPIZ payment | 888 | 11% |

FSA: Financial Social Assistance, ZPIZ: Pension and Disability Insurance Institute of Slovenia.
Note: This table compares the rate of jobseekers registered with the ESS who are temporarily non-employable, distinguishing ZPIZ recipients and recipients of social assistance. FSA recipients in this table are not limited to those identified as having a health limitation, as this information is not available. Focusing on those with health limitations only would probably yield an even higher non-employability share.
Source: OECD calculations based on European Social Survey, www.europeansocialsurvey.org/data/.

StatLink https://stat.link/vg1euc

## 4.3. The link between unemployment and sickness and disability

The only formal interaction between ZPIZ and ESS is the need for unemployed partial disability beneficiaries to register with the ESS. Other than this, the co-operation between the two institutions is rather inexistent:

- There are barely any data exchanges. For instance, neither has the ESS any information regarding ZPIZ pensions of registered jobseekers, nor is ZPIZ aware of the participation of their clients in any ESS activation programme;
- The situation is similar for other ESS activation programmes: ZPIZ recipients can participate, but the intervention of the ESS is usually coming very late, as ZPIZ recipients have to look for a job in the open labour market.

Since 2012, unemployed workers are not eligible for sickness insurance, eliminating any hitherto existing need for the ZZZS and the ESS to co-operate. Austerity Legislation (ZUJF, 2021[4]) changed the Labour Market Regulation Act (ZUTD) in a way that it abolished the right of the unemployment benefit recipients who were on the sick leave (for more than 30 working days) to receive sickness benefits at the expense of the ZZZS. Consequently, it was no possible any longer to maintain and extend unemployment benefit entitlement while on sick leave (which was possible before the Austerity law). This legislative change in 2012 applied to newly unemployed persons only, further reducing the need to co-operate across institutions.

## References

Cutler, D., A. Lleras-Muney and T. Vogl (2008), *Socioeconomic Status and Health: Dimensions and Mechanisms*, National Bureau of Economic Research, Cambridge, MA, http://dx.doi.org/10.3386/w14333. [2]

OECD (2016), *Connecting People with Jobs: The Labour Market, Activation Policies and Disadvantaged Workers in Slovenia*, Connecting People with Jobs, OECD Publishing, Paris, https://doi.org/10.1787/9789264265349-en. [1]

Vodopivec, M. et al. (2015), "The Effect of Unemployment Benefit Generosity on Unemployment Duration: Quasi-Experimental Evidence from Slovenia", *IZA discussion paper*, Vol. 9548, http://hdl.handle.net/10419/126636www.econstor.eu (accessed on 1 April 2021). [3]

ZUJF (2021), "Zakon za uravnoteženje javnih financ [Public Finance Balance Act]", *Official Gazette of the Republic of Slovenia*, No. 40/2012, http://pisrs.si/Pis.web/pregledPredpisa?id=ZAKO6388. [4]

## Notes

[1] EU-SILC data for 2019 suggest that in Slovenia, the share of persons with disability among these aged 50-69 is over 40%, while it is 11% among those aged 30-49.

# 5 Return-to-work policies in Slovenia for persons with health problems or disabilities

Vocational rehabilitation for persons with health problems or disabilities is a significant element of Slovenia's policy landscape. However, the setup is not conducive to good employment outcomes, for several reasons. These include the fact that the disability insurance and the employment service offer a very similar type of intervention under a different name for a different target group – while using the same rehabilitation providers. Well intended, vocational rehabilitation provided by the disability insurance has a strong focus on the workers previous job and employer – except that this comes at a time when workers have been away from work for years. Vocational rehabilitation of the employment service seems least effective for recipients of a partial disability benefit – again reflecting problems of late intervention. Finally, Slovenia has a considerable network of occupational physicians – but they are busy with tasks that have little impact on employment. Better outcomes of return-to-work policies now in place can only be achieved by a holistic reform, with a view towards early intervention and a much stronger connection of the actions of various stakeholders and institutions.

This section discusses all those elements in the Slovenian social protection system that contribute to helping people at risk of dropping out of employment for reasons of ill health or disability to remain in or return to the labour market. This includes vocational rehabilitation services offered during different phases of the process and employment programmes by the Employment Service of Slovenia, but also issues related to the role of employers and occupational doctors, and the timing of medical rehabilitation.

## 5.1. Overview of the return-to-work policies in Slovenia

### 5.1.1. Legal framework and organisation of vocational rehabilitation

Return to work for persons with health problems or disability is regulated in two main acts. The first is the Pension and Disability Insurance Act (ZPIZ-2), which specifies the social protection and vocational rehabilitation of persons with disability. The second is the Vocational Rehabilitation and Employment of Persons with Disability Act (ZZRZI), which comprises the assessment and employment rehabilitation of registered jobseekers with health barriers to employment.[1] National budget and special-purpose funds are the main source of income funding these programmes.

Both ZPIZ-2 and ZZRZI specify that the right to employment (re)integration only cover people with a legally confirmed disability status. A person is entitled to a legal disability status and rights derived from that status, if he or she has permanent impairments regarding work, employment, career development and employability in general. There are two ways to acquire a legal disability status (depending on the length of employment): through ZPIZ and the Pension and Disability Insurance Act for insured persons or through the ESS and the ZZRZI for unemployed persons with disability.

The legislation addresses the issue of employment of persons with disability indirectly, as it covers much broader topics of social protection as well. Under the Pension and Disability Insurance Act, the following programmes/schemes to promote the employment of persons with disability are listed (several of them covered in Chapter 1): disability allowance, compensation for disability, vocational rehabilitation, transfer to another workplace and part-time work, workplace adaptation, on-the-job training, formal and non-formal education. Under the Vocational Rehabilitation and Employment of Persons with Disability Act, the following programmes/schemes/rights are available: vocational rehabilitation, supported employment, wage subsidies, workplace adaptation, exemptions from tax and social security contribution, the award for exceeding the quota, employment in companies that are adapted for employment persons with disabilities.

Given the long-term nature of sickness leave, employment of persons with disability and health problems should also be part of the Health Care and Health Insurance Act, which regulates sickness insurance, but that is not the case. Although employers contribute the funds for occupational diseases and injuries to the health insurance, these funds are not available to rehabilitate workers on sickness leave.

The main responsible institutions for implementing vocational rehabilitation measures fall under the Ministry of Labour, Family, Social Affairs and Equal Opportunities. These are the Employment Service of Slovenia (ESS), the Pension and Disability Insurance Institute of Slovenia (ZPIZ), the Public Guarantee, Maintenance and Disability Fund of the Republic of Slovenia, the Slovenian Association of Vocational Rehabilitation Providers, the various private vocational rehabilitation providers, and the Development Centre for Vocational Rehabilitation at the University Rehabilitation Institute.

Vertical co-operation of each institution with the ministry is now common practice but horizontal co-operation among individual institutions is lacking. As a result, different programmes are not well connected and it is not possible or very difficult to switch from one to another, even in situations where this would be a good solution. For instance, employment rehabilitation and vocational rehabilitation do not offer the same services, so it would be sometimes reasonable for an individual to switch from one programme to another, but that is not possible. Multi-sectoral co-operation (e.g. between ZZZS and ZPIZ) is particularly problematic, which reflects, among others, the long duration of the various procedures.

### 5.1.2. Psychosocial programmes

Besides programmes for promoting employment of people with disability, there are other psychosocial programmes aimed at promoting inclusion and development in other life areas, not directly aimed at promoting employment. The significance of those programmes lies in raising self-esteem and quality of life in general, which can influence employment possibilities. This includes various programmes for persons with mental health problems, defined in the Mental Health Act (*Zakon o duševnem zdravju*) and the Resolution on the National Mental Health Programme (MIRA) 2018-28. MIRA is the first strategic document in the Republic of Slovenia that comprehensively addresses and regulates the field of mental health.

The programme connects existing and adds new services and structures to respond to people's mental health needs, with focus on strengthening mental health and preventing and comprehensively treating mental disorders. To this end, it connects the services of all responsible sectors, i.e. health, social care, education and training. The goal of the programme is to establish a good supportive environment in all areas of mental health care, and to bring services closer to users and encourage them to seek help early, thus reducing institutionalisation in the field of mental health.

### 5.1.3. Employed persons with disability

Legislation promotes the employment of persons with disability through various measures. For person with disability who have a job, the legislation obliges employers to an active role in solving problems in relation to employment, to reduce the risk of unemployment. However, dismissal is possible for an employer who no longer has a suitable job to offer (see below for more details).

More problems arise in the employment of people with disability in small businesses, with fewer employment possibilities due to working conditions and greater demands. In particular, there is a lack of professional support for small businesses and a less developed support network, while there are no differences in financial incentives for large or small businesses. In smaller companies, there are no professionals employed to advise the employer on the employment of people with disability. There are also fewer options for reassignment in smaller businesses in the event a person is no longer able to perform his/her job due to a disability.

There is a need to establish special centres or information points, which provide employment support for people with disability and their employers. In such centres or contact points, employers and insured persons should receive all the information on the possibilities for returning to work, regardless of the legal basis of their rights. The proposal for the organisation of such support will be one of the main outcomes of the Early Vocational Rehabilitation and Return-to-Work Process Project (see Box 5.1).

Another measure to promote employment of persons with disability is the quota system, regulated in the Vocational Rehabilitation and Employment of Persons with Disabilities Act. Employers in both public and private sector organisations employing over 20 employees have an obligation to hire a certain share of workers with disability. However, little information is available about quota fulfilment.

Employers who hire persons with disability with reduced work capacity can receive compensation from the government for the possible loss in productivity. A wage subsidy to compensate the loss in productivity is a right to which a person with disability is entitled.

Significant challenges remain in increasing employment of persons with disability. First, stigma and bias against disability prevail in workplaces and among employers, who have insufficient knowledge and information regarding employment of persons with disability and their work ability. Second, there is a shortage of adapted workplaces. Third, the quota system stipulates a quota between 2% to 6%, depending on the company's activity. The low lower boundary of 2% applicable in many sectors is unjustified and the quota to be increased in the affected sectors. This includes: wholesale and retail, repair of motor vehicles and motorcycles, accommodation and food service activities, information and communication, financial and insurance activities, professional, scientific and technical activities, public administration and defence, compulsory social security, arts, entertainment and recreation, and other service activities.

## 5.2. Vocational rehabilitation under the Pension and Disability Insurance Act

The Pension and Disability Insurance Act (ZPIZ-2) grants the right to vocational rehabilitation, in addition to the rights to compensation for disability, to transfer to another workplace, to part-time work, the rights to other allowances under disability insurance, and a right to reimbursement of travel expenses.

Recall that the precondition for acquiring any rights under the Pension and Disability Insurance Act is that the treatment and the process of medical rehabilitation is completed. The process of vocational rehabilitation as a right under this Act cannot start if the person is still waiting for surgery or other therapeutic interventions, or is involved in any form of medical rehabilitation. Due to waiting times for therapeutic interventions and rehabilitation and due to the course of the treatment itself, vocational rehabilitation is postponed even though the insured person would be able to start the process. The end of the treatment has to be declared even before an adjustment of the workplace or work environment or before a technical adaptation of the workplace. Therefore, the person cannot test the adjustment in the given circumstances and before the actual return to work happens. This is also a problem for the unemployed, because they cannot acquire the right to workplace adjustment when they get employed.

Recall also that the number of disability applicants engaging in vocational rehabilitation remains stubbornly low. Figure 3.6 in Chapter 3 showed that in 2019, 141 disability claimants participated in vocational rehabilitation, about 40% of these initially referred to vocational rehabilitation. This figure is not very optimistic on the current capacity of the system to engage disability claimants in return-to-work activities.

The 2016 White Paper on Pensions posits that a potential reason for the low take-up of vocational rehabilitation may be its poor outcomes (MDDSZ, 2016[1]). Presenting qualitative evaluations, the White Paper suggests that employers too often are not willing to maintain an employment relationship with disability claimants undergoing rehabilitation. This is the result of a lack of co-operation between employers, employees and professional rehabilitation workers. Moreover, the duration of vocational rehabilitation tends to be long, further worsening the employability of the participants. Finally, participants may fear having to reimburse the costs of vocational rehabilitation in case of unsuccessful completion.

Vocational rehabilitation most often takes the form of education or training, although adjustments of the workplace and practical work are slowly gaining importance over time. Table 5.1 shows that in 45% of the cases, vocational rehabilitation involved further education, and in 35% short-term training or education. The weight of education is declining over time, to the advantage of other forms of vocational rehabilitation such as adjustment of the workplace.

Vocational rehabilitation is available almost exclusively to young workers, in line with the strong emphasis of the programme on education and training. Figure 5.1 shows that very few beneficiaries over age 45 ever engage in vocational rehabilitation. The bulk of claimants are under age 40, apparently the age when participating in training and education (to improve employment opportunities) is considered a meaningful step, a view shared by the employers contacted during the OECD missions. Note the very similar age distribution with claimants of temporary benefits, in line with the previous evidence presented on the characteristics of the claimants of both programmes.

### Table 5.1. Vocational rehabilitation most often takes the form of education or training

Composition (in percentage) of all activities included under vocational rehabilitation by year, 2015-19

|  | Full-time education | Part-time education | Short-term training or education | On-the-job training | Adjustment of the workplace |
|---|---|---|---|---|---|
| 2019 | 45.4 | 2.1 | 34.8 | 6.4 | 11.3 |
| 2017 | 43.2 | 7.4 | 36.8 | 5.3 | 7.3 |
| 2016 | 54.8 | 1.7 | 31.3 | 6.1 | 6.1 |
| 2015 | 57.2 | 11.0 | 26.9 | 1.4 | 3.5 |

Source: OECD calculations based on Pension and Disability Insurance Institute of Slovenia (ZPIZ) data www.zpiz.si.

StatLink https://stat.link/r9b3ez

### Figure 5.1. Vocational rehabilitation is used almost exclusively by young workers

Distribution of average age of disability stock by type of benefit, 2019

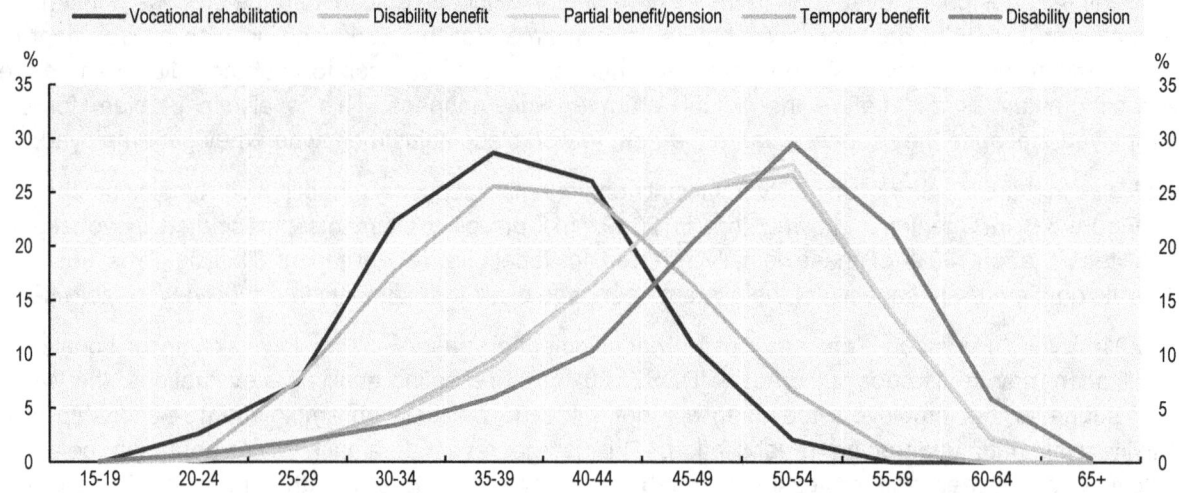

Source: OECD calculations based on Pension and Disability Insurance Institute of Slovenia (ZPIZ) data www.zpiz.si.

StatLink https://stat.link/kmfx3b

Other than the share of claimants ultimately engaging in vocational rehabilitation, there is no information to assess the effectiveness of vocational rehabilitation services. Data on the outcomes of vocational rehabilitation are not available, which makes impossible any analysis of the programmes. The OECD team has encountered substantial reservations to sharing data on vocational rehabilitation, let alone linking these data with other administrative records to analyse their effectiveness. There are also no impact evaluations of the programmes available, nor any plans to conduct them.

## 5.3. Fostering the return to work of unemployed persons with disability

### 5.3.1. Employment Rehabilitation and Employment of Persons with Disabilities Act

The previous chapter concluded that the ESS is putting significant emphasis on identifying health barriers to employment. The ESS has several tools in place to profile registered jobseekers, including a medical assessment to help caseworkers make informed decisions in cases of suspected health barriers to employment. Another tool to identify health barriers to employment are the services under the ZZRZI act. While the goal of this act is to regulate employment rehabilitation, the first step of the rehabilitation process is an assessment under the Standards for Vocational Rehabilitation Services,[2] and an opinion on the eligibility for the disability status and the right to vocational rehabilitation services. As the data show, a very relevant part of the work of the ESS through this act is to grant a legal disability status.

The ESS decides on entitlement for employment rehabilitation with help of rehabilitation providers. Rehabilitation providers send an opinion to the ESS, where the Rehabilitation Commission decides upon an assessment of the opinion of the provider. The ESS has to issue a decision on the status of a person with disability and the right to employment rehabilitation, before referral to employment rehabilitation. The ESS rehabilitation counsellor in co-operation with the person with disability defines the plan of rehabilitation with a set of appropriate services.

Employment rehabilitation services aim to prepare persons with disability for a new job. Service users gain better insight into their abilities and strengths, get to know their limits and become aware of the available support for performing their work. They can redefine their career goals and gain an understanding of the knowledge, skills, and experience required for a job. Services target the development of social skills as well as work-related skills. The interdisciplinary rehabilitation team can provide assistance as required including psychosocial support, vocational guidance and job-search assistance. Successful employment rehabilitation requires the co-operation of employers and can include workplace and work environment analysis and adjustments, on-the-job training, and professional support in the workplace.

*Two pieces of legislation for one type of intervention*

Two parallel legislations on rehabilitation are reflective of the disconnection of the system. While, effectively, rehabilitation services offered under ZPIZ-2 and ZZRZI are quite similar, there is not a single act serving as umbrella legislation for the employment of persons with disabilities. The government has adopted several documents to promote employment of persons with disability, regardless of the type of disability, but divided the support by individual organisational units, with a lack of co-operation among them. While the legislation under the ZZRZI is coherent and compatible, there is no link to the ZPIZ-2 in the field of vocational rehabilitation.

The legislation brings a dichotomy in the services and treatment offered to those eligible for disability insurance and those not eligible. There is a gap in the national legislation between the employment needs of persons with reduced work capacity and legal provisions on their professional (re)integration, between ZPIZ-2 and ZZRZI:

- Psychosocial services and supported employment services are recognised and enabled only for persons with disability included in the rehabilitation process under the ZZRZI;
- While the ZZRZI provides a wider range of services, it does not provide payment for education, which is possible in principle for all unemployed persons through the Active Labour Market Programmes offered by the ESS but depends on the annual budget;
- On the contrary, ZPIZ-2 cover education services while it otherwise offers a smaller range of rights regarding employment (work place adaptation, formal and informal education, training for new profession), excluding psychosocial and supported employment services.

A key difference between vocational rehabilitation (ZPIZ) and employment rehabilitation (ZZRZI) is the role played by employers. Employers play a major role in the process of vocational rehabilitation as specified under ZPIZ-2: the purpose of rehabilitation is to find a job with the same employer, and employers may prevent their employees from engaging in vocational rehabilitation if they cannot offer a suitable job under any circumstances. Employment rehabilitation under the ZZRZI targets unemployed persons with disability, with the aim to help them in finding a new job that accommodates their disability.

*Employment rehabilitation providers*

A network of rehabilitation providers offers employment rehabilitation services. This network consists of 14 providers that operate throughout the country. One of them is a public institution while all others are private organisations with public service concession. Providers unite in the Slovenian Association of Vocational Rehabilitation Providers, which operates on the national level. Each service provider within the network of providers operates on the regional and local level to respect the principle of equal access.

All rehabilitation providers provide the same services. They must provide all vocational rehabilitation services in accordance with the standards. The law also determines the composition of the expert teams which include different professionals, including occupational therapists, psychologists, social workers and other profiles of social sciences, humanities (e.g. pedagogues) and technical fields (e.g. rehabilitation technologists). A specialist in occupational, traffic and sports medicine is required. Vocational rehabilitation services for the blind and partially sighted are provided only by URI-Soča and for the deaf and hard of hearing only by Racio. They both provide services throughout Slovenia as a mobile team.

Every vocational rehabilitation provider is obliged to develop a network of employers. This provides a set of possibilities to reach the most optimal conditions for specific workplaces or selected professions, with the aim to ensure the improvement of employment opportunities for persons with disability. The network includes regular employers and employers who employ under special conditions (employment centres and companies specialised in employing persons with disability).[3] In the current network of active employers, as in previous years, most companies were from the regular work environment, followed by employment centres and companies specialised in employing persons with disability. Co-operation with associations, institutes and social enterprises is not negligible either.

Long waiting times of providers is an issue, even after completion of the assessment of disability. As discussed above, medical assessments to identify health barriers to employment typically happen long after the start of unemployment spells. This is the result of long waiting periods at many vocational rehabilitation providers, varying greatly across providers (between one week and 15 months). The long waiting time between the decision on acquired disability rights and the referral to vocational rehabilitation services is problematic for many, as both motivation and employability drop over time.

*Quality control*

The Development Centre for Vocational Rehabilitation at the University Rehabilitation Institute is responsible for drawing up quality standards in the area of vocational rehabilitation, using European Quality in Social Services (EQUASS) standards. EQUASS aims to enhance the social service sector by engaging service providers in quality, continuous improvement, learning, and development, to guarantee service users high the quality of services throughout Europe. The EQUASS standards comprises ten quality principles (Leadership, Staff, Rights, Ethics, Partnership, Participation, Person-centred approach, Comprehensiveness, Result Orientation, Continuous improvement), broken down into detailed quality criteria (in total, about 50 criteria). Specific performance indicators measure the performance according to the quality criteria. Those principles, criteria, and indicators must be taken into account while implementing the EQUASS standards and striving for valid and relevant results for EQUASS Assurance or EQUASS Excellence recognition by the European Quality for Social Services.

The network of vocational rehabilitation providers in Slovenia follows EQUASS standards since 2010 (at URI-Soča, since 2007). The Ministry of Labour, Family, Social Affairs and Equal Opportunities strongly supports the EQUASS quality standards. Note that vocational rehabilitation providers in Slovenia use EQUASS standards also for the services provided under the Pension and Disability Insurance Act.

*Outcomes of employment rehabilitation*

Around 1900 jobseekers are included in employment rehabilitation every year (Table 5.2). This number, which has remained more or less constant during the past decade, includes jobseekers with disability regardless of the type of their disability (including mental health, physical, intellectual, and/or sensory impairments). According to the provisions of the network of rehabilitation providers, the annual norm is around 1980 treated persons per year, or between 100 and 120 rehabilitees per rehabilitation team, an average of 110 persons per professional team (referred by the ESS).

There is substantial regional variation in the take up rate of employment rehabilitation, compared to the number of unemployed with disability. Across Slovenia, 15% of jobseekers identified as having a recognised disability are included in employment rehabilitation. This share ranges from as low as 8% of these jobseekers in Sevnica to 22% in Velenje and Nova Gorica. The number of jobseekers participating in employment rehabilitation over the total number of jobseekers ranges from 2-5%, not entirely in line with the shares of participation over identified jobseekers with disability (Table 5.2).

The large majority of assessments issued by the Rehabilitation Committee classify employment rehabilitation participants as unemployable. Participants who do not transition to the open labour market are classified by the Rehabilitation Committee according to their degree of employability. Table 5.2 shows that, nationally, 69% of participants are assessed unemployable after completion of the vocational rehabilitation programme, 17% could work in protected or sheltered employment, and 14% in supported regular employment. There is large variation in these shares across ESS regions, in line with the availability of establishments of supported and/or protected employment. For instance, in Novo Mesto, 62% of participants are employable under supported employment, while this share is 4% in Maribor and Murska Sobota. The share of protected employment varies a little less across regions, still ranging from 30% in Ljubljana to 4% in Trbovlje and Velenje. Underdeveloped supported and protected employment systems result in high shares of assessments as "unemployable", which in turn prevents these jobseekers from being further activated.

About 27% of the participants in employment rehabilitation transition to any form of employment (Table 5.3). The employability assessment of the Rehabilitation Commission provides only a partial picture of the outcomes of employment rehabilitation. More interesting is how many jobseekers actually transition to employment after participating in employment rehabilitation. Data show that the transition rate is largest for jobseekers with a legal disability status (32%), followed by jobseekers obtaining a disability status through the ZZRZI (30%). Partial disability beneficiaries are benefitting the least from employment rehabilitation. The high rate of transition to employment for holders of a legal disability status may be surprising at first, as these persons usually have congenital and more severe disabilities. Given that there is no obligation for holders of a legal disability status to register with the ESS, those observed in this analysis are possibly a selected sample, with a particular interest in and capacity to work. The poor performance of partial ZPIZ beneficiaries partly is a result of the structure of the employment rehabilitation system for ZPIZ recipients, as described in more detail below. Until the 2021 amendment of the ZZRZI, recipients of partial ZPIZ benefits did not receive remuneration for their work when working through the system of employment rehabilitation. The 2021 amendment removed this dichotomy, allowing recipients of partial ZPIZ benefits to receive financial incentives, incentivising ZPIZ recipients to fully engage with, and benefit from, employment rehabilitation.

### Table 5.2. The majority of assessments classify employment rehabilitation participants as unemployable

Participation in employment rehabilitation and employability assessment (issued decisions by the Rehabilitation Committee) after participation, 2019

|  | Participants in employment rehabilitation | | | Employability status after participation in employment rehabilitation (% of all employment rehabilitation participants) | | |
|---|---|---|---|---|---|---|
|  | Total in 2019 | In percentage of jobseekers with disability | In percentage of total number of unemployed | Supported employment | Protected employment | Unemployable |
| *Slovenia* | *1 909* | *15%* | *3%* | *14%* | *17%* | *69%* |
| Celje | 164 | 10% | 2% | 25% | 17% | 58% |
| Koper | 77 | 9% | 2% | 34% | 19% | 47% |
| Kranj | 103 | 19% | 2% | 29% | 19% | 51% |
| Ljubljana | 404 | 14% | 2% | 14% | 30% | 56% |
| Maribor | 215 | 18% | 2% | 4% | 19% | 77% |
| Murska Sobota | 224 | 13% | 4% | 4% | 10% | 86% |
| Nova Gorica | 123 | 22% | 4% | 13% | 14% | 73% |
| Novo Mesto | 121 | 15% | 3% | 62% | 24% | 14% |
| Ptuj | 97 | 21% | 4% | 7% | 24% | 69% |
| Sevnica | 67 | 8% | 2% | 23% | 23% | 54% |
| Trbovlje | 71 | 20% | 3% | 33% | 4% | 63% |
| Velenje | 243 | 22% | 5% | 17% | 4% | 79% |

Note: Table shows decisions issued by the Rehabilitation Commission, not including all exits from employment rehabilitation. Some jobseekers leave to the open labour market, while others may drop out of rehabilitation entirely. Information on these shares is not available.
Source: OECD calculations based on European Social Survey, www.europeansocialsurvey.org/data/.

StatLink https://stat.link/3wb6zp

### Table 5.3. About 27% of participants in employment rehabilitation transition to employment

Referrals to employment rehabilitation and outflow to employment by disability status, 2018-19

|  | Legal disability status | ZZRZI status | Partial ZPIZ recipients | Total |
|---|---|---|---|---|
| Referred jobseekers | 376 | 2 628 | 939 | 3 943 |
| Outflow to employment | 121 | 792 | 156 | 1 069 |
| Rate of employment | 32% | 30% | 16% | 27% |

ZZRZI: Vocational Rehabilitation and Employment of Persons with Disability, ZPIZ: Pension and Disability Institute of Slovenia.
Note: ZZRZI status indicates these jobseekers obtaining a recognition of their disability through the ZZRZI act.
Source: OECD calculations based on European Social Survey, www.europeansocialsurvey.org/data/.

StatLink https://stat.link/3kltx4

The share of jobseekers still unemployed after participating in employment rehabilitation increases with the duration of unemployment before entry in the programme (Table 5.4). Of those jobseekers entering employment rehabilitation in the second year of their unemployment spell, only 8% remain unemployed. This share increases to 16% for those entering in their third year, to 26% in the fourth, and to 50% for those participating after 5 years or more of unemployment. This dramatic increase with the length of unemployment calls for early vocational rehabilitation as a means to reduce unemployment. In this context, it is worth emphasising that participating in the first year of unemployment is not happening, because of both the long waiting times at vocational rehabilitation providers, and the large caseloads for ESS caseworkers: early activation, at present, means intervening in the second year of unemployment.

Vocational rehabilitation providers note the increasing complexity of their cases, which sometimes have to go through Social Inclusion Programmes first. The employment of people with mental health problems, the increase in demands of employers and the increase in complexity of health problems are among the biggest problems for employment rehabilitation. Unemployable persons with disability have the right to participate in the Social Inclusion Programme funded by Ministry of Labour, Family, Social Affairs and Equal Opportunities. These are special programmes designed to support and maintain the working abilities of persons with disability, implemented by special providers selected via a public tender for a period of four years. It is possible to transfer from the Social Inclusion Programme to employment, but such transfers are an exception.

Table 5.4. The share of jobseekers still unemployed after participating in employment rehabilitation increases with the length of the unemployment spell before entry into the programme

Still unemployed after participation in employment rehabilitation by duration of unemployment, 2018-19

|  | 12-23 months | 24-35 months | 36-59 months | 60+ months |
| --- | --- | --- | --- | --- |
| Legal disability | 14% | 18% | 22% | 47% |
| ZPIZ | 7% | 15% | 25% | 53% |
| ZZRZI | 8% | 17% | 28% | 47% |
| Total | 8% | 16% | 26% | 50% |

ZPIZ: Pension and Disability Insurance Institute of Slovenia. ZZRZI: Vocational Rehabilitation and Employment of Persons with Disability.
Source: OECD calculations based on European Social Survey, https://www.europeansocialsurvey.org/data/.

StatLink https://stat.link/59jmnr

### 5.3.2. Labour market programmes for jobseekers with disability

In addition to participating in employment rehabilitation, persons with disability can participate in Active Labour Market Programmes (ALMPs), non-specifically tailored for persons with disability. These programmes are aimed at all unemployed people and their availability depends on the resources available. The choice of participants to these programmes does not depend on their health conditions. ALMPs can take the form of training and education, employment subsidies, job creation measures, self-employment subsidies, among many others.

ZPIZ beneficiaries are overrepresented among participants in job creation programmes, in line with the greater employability challenges they face (Table 5.5). Public works programmes aim at stimulating and developing new workplaces or preserving current ones, and developing the working ability of unemployed people. These programmes are organised to conduct social, educational, cultural, environmental, municipal, agricultural and other measures (Južnik Rotar, 2011[2]). These programmes target jobseekers facing health barriers to employment compounded by social exclusion and other social challenges.

The effectiveness of ALMPs is lower for ZPIZ recipients than for other jobseekers. This is not surprising, as jobseekers receiving ZPIZ benefits have a lower employability than the average jobseeker. Despite participating in ALMPs, lacking labour demand may hinder a transition to the open labour market. Figure 5.2 shows the share of ALMP participants that do not transition to employment after participating in ALMPs, by duration since programme participation. A much smaller share of jobseekers receiving ZPIZ benefits transitions to employment than for the average jobseeker. Comparing ZPIZ and FSA recipients, the difference is less striking, however. During the first month after participating in an ALMP, a very similar share of ZPIZ recipients and FSA recipients among jobseekers transition to employment. For ZPIZ recipients, the transition to employment plateaus quickly (see the kink in the curve after the first month after programme completion), while employment transitions mildly continue for FSA jobseekers.

Table 5.5. ZPIZ beneficiaries are overrepresented in job-creation programmes

Participation in ALMP programmes by ALMP category for all jobseekers, FSA and ZPIZ beneficiaries, 2019

| ALMP category | Specific programmes | All jobseekers | FSA beneficiaries | ZPIZ beneficiaries |
| --- | --- | --- | --- | --- |
| Training and education | Institutional training, Non-formal training, On the job training, Job trial, Project learning for young adults, National vocational qualifications, Non formal training for migrants | 49% | 65% | 34% |
| Employment subsidies | Employ.me, Sustainable employment for young unemployed, tax and contribution reduction for employment vulnerable unemployed | 32% | 13% | 22% |
| Job creation (Public works) | Public works, Public works – helping migrants, Learning workshops: training + employment subsidy | 17% | 21% | 44% |
| Self-employment subsidies | Self-employment subsidy | 1% | 1% | 0% |
| *Total jobseekers* | | *103 641* | *8 560* | *8 944* |

ALMP: Active Labour Market Programme. FSA: Financial Social Assistance, ZPIZ: Pension and Disability Insurance Institute of Slovenia.
Source: OECD calculations based on European Social Survey, https://www.europeansocialsurvey.org/data/.

StatLink https://stat.link/fnc7to

Figure 5.2. The effectiveness of ALMPs is lower for ZPIZ recipients than for other jobseekers

Share of ALMP participants not transitioning to employment after participating, 2019

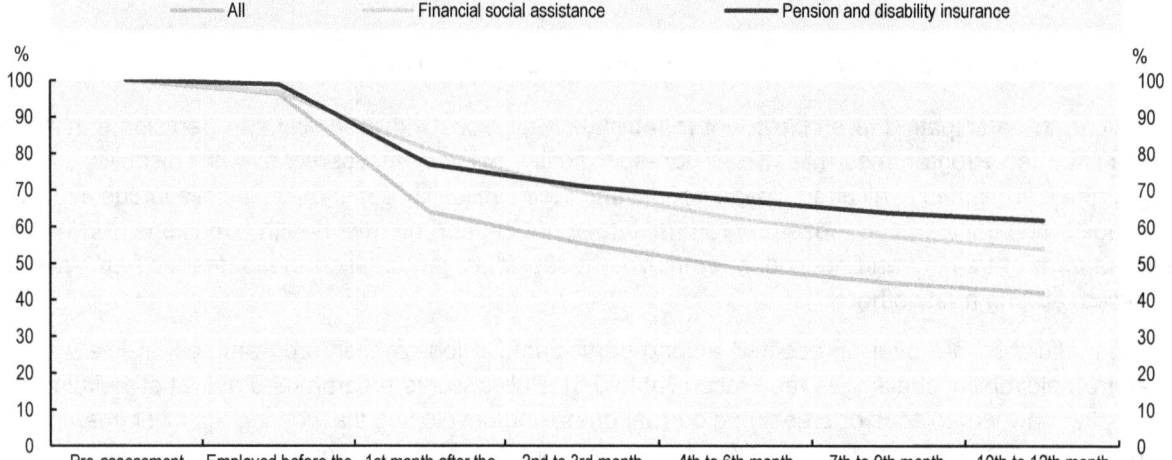

ALMP: Active Labour Market Programme, ZPIZ: Pension and Disability Insurance Institute of Slovenia.
Note: The share of transitions to employment is constructed from raw data, mimicking a survival probability analysis. Prior to being on an ALMP, no participant was employed (i.e. the share that has not transitioned to employment=100%). As transitions to employment occur, this share is recalculated, by time since participating in an ALMP, taking into account the persons who have not transitioned to employment.
Source: OECD calculations based on European Social Survey, www.europeansocialsurvey.org/data/.

StatLink https://stat.link/7saibf

ZPIZ beneficiaries participate in ALMPs much later than the average jobseeker, in line with a push to have these beneficiaries find a job independently in the open labour market. Table 5.6 illustrates that 53% of all jobseekers participate in ALMPs in the first five months of an unemployment spell. This figure drops to around one in four for jobseekers receiving FSA or ZPIZ benefits, possibly due to the stronger activation requirements for unemployment benefit recipients. For FSA recipients, contrary to regular jobseekers, participation in ALMPs is largely independent of the duration of unemployment. The most striking finding for ZPIZ recipients among jobseekers is the very high share of them (48%) participating in ALMPs only after having been unemployed for at least two years. These data are in line with ESS experts' views that recipients of ZPIZ benefits do not have sufficient incentives to participate in ALMPs. This figure is even higher when looking at participation in employment rehabilitation: 80% of jobseekers receiving ZPIZ benefits enter employment rehabilitation only after two years of unemployment. According to ESS experts, this is the result of a practice expecting from beneficiaries of partial disability benefits to find a job by themselves in the open labour market.

Table 5.6. ZPIZ beneficiaries participate in ALMPs much later than the average jobseeker

Participants in ALMPs by unemployment spell before participation and source of income support, 2019

|  | All jobseekers | Share | FSA beneficiaries | Share | ZPIZ beneficiaries | Share |
| --- | --- | --- | --- | --- | --- | --- |
| 0-5 months | 14 592 | 53% | 2 033 | 25% | 267 | 26% |
| 6-11 months | 3 778 | 14% | 1 661 | 20% | 83 | 8% |
| 12-23 months | 4 918 | 18% | 2 194 | 27% | 174 | 17% |
| 24+ months | 4 135 | 15% | 2 345 | 28% | 485 | 48% |

ALMPs: Active Labour Market Programmes, ZPIZ: Pension and Disability Insurance Institute of Slovenia.
Source: OECD calculations based on European Social Survey, www.europeansocialsurvey.org/data/.

StatLink https://stat.link/ajsmy4

ALMPs are most effective in returning people to work early in the unemployment spell. Early help is more likely to have an impact on subsequent employment. The effectiveness of ALMPs decreases as the pre-participation unemployment spell increases. Jobseekers participating in ALMPs in the first five months of their unemployment spell are twice as likely to find employment one month after completion of the programme as jobseekers with 24+ months of unemployment (Figure 5.3). This strongly aligns with findings from research which has established that early intervention is more effective than late intervention (Card, Kluve and Weber, 2010[3]). The policy recommendations from this finding are clear: activation and ALMP participation should kick in as early as possible in the unemployment spell.

Figure 5.3. ALMPs are most effective when participation happens early in the unemployment spell

Transition to employment after participation in ALMP, by main source of income and timing of intervention, 2017-20

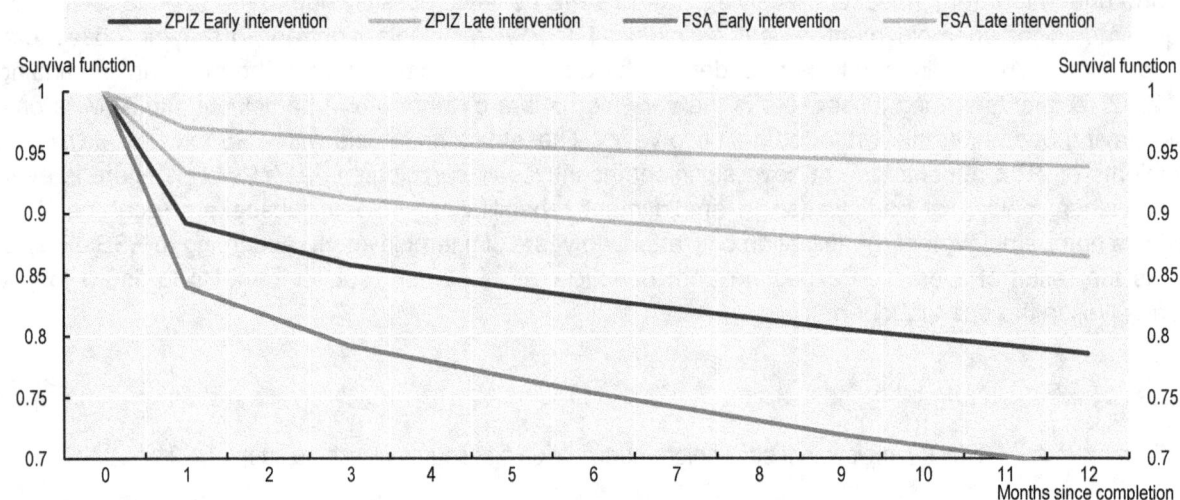

ALMP: Active Labour Market Programme. FSA: Financial Social Assistance. ZPIZ: Pension and Disability Insurance Institute of Slovenia.
Note: The survival function is calculated using a Cox proportional hazard model including the type of main source of income support (FSA, ZPIZ, and other), the months of unemployment before participation in ALMP (0-5 months, 6-12 months, 13-23 months, 24 and more), and an interaction between the two. Early intervention is the survival function for jobseekers participating in ALMPs within the first five months of unemployment spell, while late intervention is that for jobseekers participating after 24 months.
Source: OECD calculations based on European Social Survey, www.europeansocialsurvey.org/data/.

StatLink ⟶ https://stat.link/zy0x84

The low effectiveness of ALMPs for ZPIZ recipients forces rethinking the current process. Figure 5.2 shows that ZPIZ recipients respond less to ALMPs than the average jobseeker. While this may be because ZPIZ recipients have a lower degree of employability, it may also partly be a consequence of their late activation.

### 5.3.3. Comparison of the effectiveness of the different types of interventions

One in four partial ZPIZ beneficiaries participate in an ESS programme, in one of three ways: through a medical assessment, employment rehabilitation, or ALMP participation. ZPIZ recipients participating in ALMPs have higher relative educational attainment than those included in medical assessments, but have a similar age distribution (Table 5.7). The age distribution of participants is different from that of participants in employment rehabilitation, who tend to be younger.

ZPIZ beneficiaries seeking work more often enter employment after participating in ALMPs than after employment rehabilitation. Employment rehabilitation facilitates a transition to work less often than the participation in employment rehabilitation, with significant differences by age in the use of the different types of interventions (Figure 5.4). Inclusions into medical assessment rarely are a followed directly by a switch into employment. There are several potential explanations for these differences in age-specific patterns in the take-up of services offered by the ESS:

- There are compositional differences in participants to different types of interventions, as seen in Table 5.7. Notably, ALMP participants have a relatively higher skill level, increasing their chances in the labour market. This would bias the results into showing a relatively higher effectiveness of ALMPs over employment rehabilitation and medical assessment.

- The system is organised such that ZPIZ recipients are included in medical assessments and employment rehabilitation as a last resort, only if they do not manage to find a job in the open labour market. The nature of the health barriers of those included in medical assessment and employment rehabilitation is thus probably more severe than that of recipients included in ALMPs.
- As a result, while it is true that participation in ALMPs happens quite late for ZPIZ recipients, inclusion in medical assessment happens even later. Almost 80% of inclusions to medical assessment take place after 24 months of unemployment (compared to 48% for ALMPs) and only 3% are included in medical assessments in the first five months of unemployment (compared to 26% for ALMPs). In line with the evidence that early intervention is key, these differences in timing of intervention could be driving part of the results.

Table 5.7. One-quarter of partial ZPIZ beneficiaries are activated by an ESS programme

Share of ZPIZ claimants included in different programmes by claimant characteristics, 2018-19

|  | Medical assessment | Participation in employment rehabilitation | Participation in ALMP |
| --- | --- | --- | --- |
| Primary school and less | 4% |  | 8% |
| Vocational education | 5% |  | 13% |
| Secondary education | 4% |  | 24% |
| Tertiary education | 3% |  | 28% |
| Men | 4% | 5% | 12% |
| Women | 4% | 7% | 15% |
| 25-29 years | 5% | 38% | 19% |
| 30-34 years | 6% | 38% | 33% |
| 35-39 years | 5% | 15% | 23% |
| 40-44 years | 5% | 14% | 23% |
| 45-49 years | 5% | 11% | 21% |
| 50-54 years | 5% | 7% | 16% |
| 55-59 years | 4% | 3% | 11% |
| 60-64 years | 2% | 1% | 4% |
| Total | 4% | 6% | 14% |

ZPIZ: Pension and Disability Insurance Institute of Slovenia.
Source: OECD calculations based on European Social Survey, https://www.europeansocialsurvey.org/data/.

StatLink https://stat.link/lmx3b7

Figure 5.4. ZPIZ beneficiaries most often enter employment after having participated in ALMPs

Share of outflows to employment of partial ZPIZ beneficiaries by type of programme and age, 2019

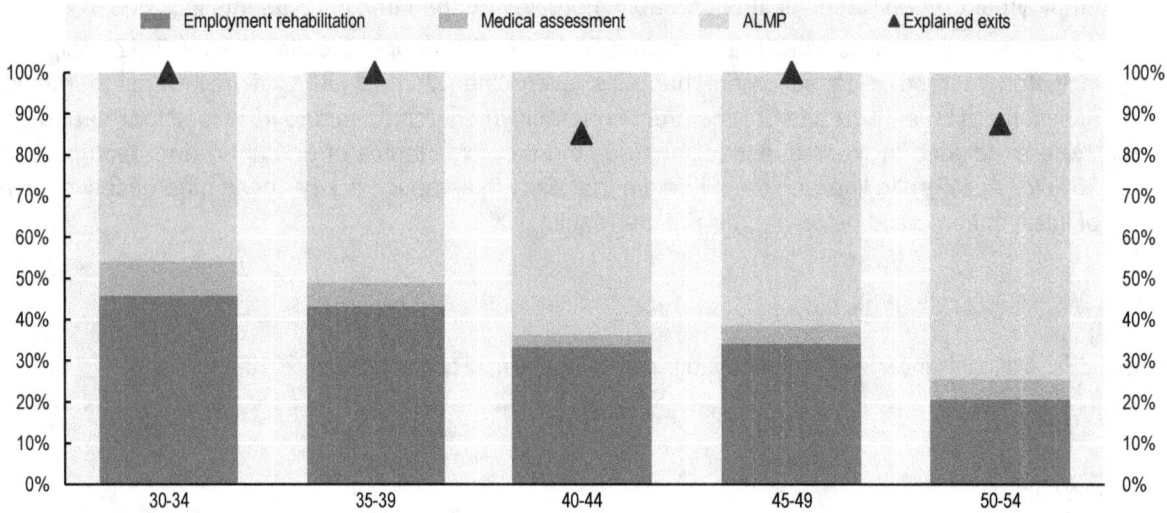

ALMP: Active Labour Market Programme. ZPIZ: Pension and Disability Insurance Institute of Slovenia.
Note: Shares are calculated as the outflows from unemployment to employment in 2019 by intervention type over the total outflow to employment of all partial ZPIZ beneficiaries in 2019. Explained exits are the sum of all exits by intervention type over the total outflow: a value lower than 100 indicates that not all persons exiting unemployment can be traced back. For medical assessment and ALMP programmes, outflows to employment are the sum of all outflows for up to a year after participation, without taking into account re-entry to unemployment.
Source: OECD calculations based on European Social Survey, ww.europeansocialsurvey.org/data/.

StatLink 🖵 https://stat.link/z5dfun

To assess the relative effectiveness of one intervention over the other, it is necessary to conduct a proper impact evaluation of the different programmes, either making use of individual-level administrative data in a regression-based analysis, or by evaluating the programmes in a randomised controlled trial. At present, there is no more in-depth evidence available than the one provided in this report.

## 5.4. Medical and vocational rehabilitation at URI-Soča

The possibility to vocational rehabilitation during long-term sick leave is available only for those insured persons included in medical rehabilitation in URI-Soča. Vocational rehabilitation at URI-Soča is an integral part of ZZZS-funded medical rehabilitation, not mentioned specifically in the legislation. Insured workers are on sickness leave at the time of treatment, and referred to the programme by GPs and other medical specialists. The outcome of this programme can be a gradual return to work or a proposal for the assessment of working capacity at the Pension and Disability Insurance Institute.

A rehabilitation team, from the Vocational Rehabilitation Centre (CPR), assesses the compatibility of the remaining functions of injured/ill people with the burden in their workplaces. The rehabilitation team consists of a doctor, a specialist in occupational, traffic and sport medicine, a psychologist, a specialist in clinical psychology, an occupational therapist, a social worker, a rehabilitation technologist and other experts, such as inclusive teaching methods in the treatment of blind and partially sighted people with disabilities. This set up is similar to the teams set up in other institutions providing vocational rehabilitation. Part of the work of the expert team is to meet with employers, and present them their employees' functional limitations and suggest appropriate work adjustments.

Those undergoing vocational rehabilitation at the CPR represent a small fraction of long-term sickness claimants. In 2020, 475 employees were included in the CPR for vocational rehabilitation (Table 5.8); of these, 84 were in a hospital in Ljubljana. Hospitalizations are available to those insured workers who cannot come for treatment on a daily basis due to a health impairment or the distance to their place of residence. This is only a small share of potential people, taking into account that in 2019 there were more than 8 000 people on sick leave for more than one year in Slovenia. Therefore, the extension of professional activities to the primary level of health care would be necessary.

Almost two-thirds of CPR participants suffer from mental, musculoskeletal or cardiovascular diseases (Table 5.8). However, there are big differences in the structure of diagnoses across the centres of Maribor and Ljubljana.[4] The main reason is that most of the people referred for vocational rehabilitation in Ljubljana are previously included in medical rehabilitation at URI-Soča, so people with cardiovascular diseases (stroke condition) predominate. In Maribor, many people come with a referral from their GP and mental health diseases predominate.

### Table 5.8. Almost two-thirds of Vocational Rehabilitation Centre participants have a mental, musculoskeletal or cardiovascular disease

Main diagnosis of patients included in vocational rehabilitation at the Vocational Rehabilitation Centre, URI-Soča, 2020

| ICD code | CPR LJ | (%) | CPR MB | (%) | CPR Total | (%) |
|---|---|---|---|---|---|---|
| F – mental and behavioural disorders | 9 | 3.5 | 86 | 39.8 | 95 | 20.0 |
| I – diseases of circulatory system | 69 | 26.6 | 22 | 10.2 | 91 | 19.2 |
| M – diseases of the musculoskeletal system and connective tissue | 53 | 20.5 | 37 | 17.1 | 90 | 18.9 |
| S, T – injuries, poisonings, other consequences of external causes | 38 | 14.7 | 14 | 6.5 | 52 | 10.9 |
| G – diseases of the nervous system | 37 | 14.3 | 13 | 6.0 | 50 | 10.5 |
| H – eye and ear diseases | 7 | 2.7 | 10 | 4.6 | 17 | 3.6 |
| C – neoplasms | 12 | 4.6 | 3 | 1.4 | 15 | 3.2 |
| D – diseases of the blood and blood-forming organs | 9 | 3.5 | 4 | 1.9 | 13 | 2.7 |
| Q – congenital malformations and deformations | 9 | 3.5 | 3 | 1.4 | 12 | 2.5 |
| R – other | 7 | 2.7 | 2 | 0.9 | 9 | 1.9 |
| J – diseases of respiratory system | 1 | 0.4 | 7 | 3.2 | 8 | 1.7 |
| E – endocrine, nutritional and metabolic diseases | 0 | 0.0 | 7 | 3.2 | 7 | 1.5 |
| Z – factors influencing health status | 2 | 0.8 | 4 | 1.9 | 6 | 1.3 |
| K – diseases of digestive system | 1 | 0.4 | 3 | 1.4 | 4 | 0.8 |
| A – certain infectious and parasitic diseases | 4 | 1.5 | 0 | 0.0 | 4 | 0.8 |
| L – diseases of the skin and subcutaneous tissue | 1 | 0.4 | 1 | 0.5 | 2 | 0.4 |
| TOTAL | 259 | 100 | 216 | 100 | 475 | 100 |

Note: ICD: International Classification of Diseases. Vocational Rehabilitation Center (CPR) in Ljubljana (LJ) and Maribor (MB).
Source: OECD calculations based on University Rehabilitation Institute Republic of Slovenia (URI-Soča) data www.ir-rs.si/.

StatLink https://stat.link/k0c296

Almost half of the participants in CPR with mental health diseases are employable, either directly or with workplace adaptations (Table 5.9). While these outcomes are not fully comparable to the decisions issued after participation in employment rehabilitation under the ZZRZI, the employment outlook for CPR participants is much more positive. There are several reasons that could be causing this, starting with differences in the severity of disability and type of diagnosis, but also the timing of intervention. CPR participants are typically on sickness leave for only several months and less than a year before starting treatment. ZPIZ claimants, on the other hand, have to complete medical treatment before participating in any vocational rehabilitation. The much earlier intervention could be instrumental in the success of vocational rehabilitation to promote the employment of persons with disability. The need for early intervention is the objective behind the current ESF-funded project with the Ministry of Labour, Family, Social Affairs and Equal Opportunities (see Box 5.1).

Most participants not returning to employment make a claim to ZPIZ or ESS under the Vocational Rehabilitation and Employment of Persons with Disabilities Act (ZZRZI). One in five CPR participants apply for a ZPIZ disability pension, considered unemployable. The remaining 27.8% transfer to the ESS, to receive support in finding employment. Very few people move on to further education. This analysis shows that the treatment usually shows the need for long-term support and co-operation across institutions providing vocational rehabilitation, and in particular, with the ESS.

Table 5.9. One in two participants to CPR are employable, directly or with workplace adaptations

Outcomes to vocational rehabilitation treatment for participants with mental health issues, 2010-11

|  | Total | Outcomes of Vocational Rehabilitation treatment | | | | | |
|---|---|---|---|---|---|---|---|
|  |  | Employable without restrictions | Able to work part-time | Able to work full-time with workplace adaptations | Further education | Unemployable (ZPIZ disability pension) | Referred to ZZRZI |
| Number of participants with mental health issues | 133 | 10 | 18 | 33 | 5 | 28 | 39 |
| Share of mental health issues (%) | 100 | 7 | 14 | 25 | 4 | 21 | 29 |
| Average age (years) | 40.8 |  |  |  |  |  |  |
| Average contributory period (years) | 16.5 |  |  |  |  |  |  |

CPR: Vocational Rehabilitation Center. ZPIZ: Pension and Disability Institute of Slovenia. ZZRZI: Vocational Rehabilitation and Employment of Persons with Disability.
Source: OECD calculations based on University Rehabilitation Institute Republic of Slovenia (URI-Soča) data www.ir-rs.si/.

StatLink https://stat.link/d95fwp

> **Box 5.1. The Early Vocational Rehabilitation in the Return-to-Work Process Project as a solution to a low return-to-work rate**
>
> **ESF-Funded project on early vocational rehabilitation**
>
> To tackle the issues regarding the long duration of sick leaves, the low percentage of insured people that assert their right to vocational rehabilitation, and the lack of co-operation of the key institutions in the return-to-work process, the Ministry of Labour, Family, Social Affairs and Equal Opportunities proposed a project to improve the return-to-work process in Slovenia.
>
> The Early Vocational Rehabilitation in the Return-to-Work Process Project started in May 2020 and running until December 2022. The project aims to seek solutions, which will serve as the basis for further implementations of systemic changes in practice. The project is managed by URI-Soča in co-operation with various stakeholders, including the Ministry of Labour, Family, Social Affairs and Equal Opportunities, the Ministry of Health, the Pension and Disability Insurance Institute of Slovenia, the Health Insurance Institute of Slovenia, providers of vocational rehabilitation services, occupational, traffic and sports medicine specialists, employers and insured persons. The project is co-financed by the Republic of Slovenia and the European Union, through the European Social Fund.
>
> The activities of the Early Vocational Rehabilitation in the Return-to-Work Process project focus on solving employment problems of persons with reduced work capacity. The purpose of the project is to reform the current model of vocational rehabilitation into a comprehensive early vocational rehabilitation in the return-to-work process, with focus on promoting co-operation between all the participating stakeholders in the return-to-work process. The project will address system deficiencies, such as lack of connection between medical and vocational rehabilitation, differences in the two vocational rehabilitation programmes, and lack of comprehensive information on both vocational rehabilitation and the return-to-work process. Based on the results of the pilot implementation of the new vocational rehabilitation model, the project will propose new systemic solutions. The project results will thus help preventing early exit from the labour market, especially of persons who had been absent from work long-term due to illness or disability.
>
> Source: University Rehabilitation Institute Republic of Slovenia (URI-Soča) data www.ir-rs.si/.

Among participants with mental health conditions, there are notable differences in the outcomes of vocational rehabilitation. In the case of organic mental disorders, the proposal for retirement or unemployment is most common; in schizophrenia, personality disorders and mental retardation, the most common suggestion is employment rehabilitation under the ZZRZI and in personality disorders also the ability to work full-time with restrictions. Ability to work full-time but with restrictions is also the most common suggestion in mood and neurotic disorders.

There has been a gradual shift in the role of the CPR, from being the basis for assessment at ZPIZ to providing complete return-to-work services. In 2010, a targeted study showed that the ZPIZ board fully endorses 64% of CPR opinions and summarises them in its own opinion. In recent years, CPR has completely shifted to the return-to-work process and is trying to introduce good practice in this area.

## 5.5. The role of employers and occupational physicians

### 5.5.1. Employers have unusual roles in the Slovenian system

Employers are fully responsible for ensuring health and safety at work. They have to involve occupational medicine specialists and safety at work engineers in certain tasks, but the ultimate responsibility remains entirely with the employer.

*The role of employers during sick leave*

During each sick leave, the employer has to pay the employee's wage for 30 working days. After this period, the Health Insurance Institute of Slovenia takes over continued wage payments. In Slovenia, the incidence of sick leave in 2019 was 4.6%, of which 2.1% was at the expense of employers and 2.5% at the expense of the ZZZS. Employers have no special obligation to maintain contact with a worker who is on sick leave. There are protocols on who the worker must inform that he is absent from work (usually the immediate superior or the human resources department). In the past, employees themselves had to deliver a sickness certificate from their GP to the company but since 2020, employers receive information on approved sick leave online. It thus now depends on the level of communication within the company, if the employee reports a sickness absence at all.

When the payment of compensation transfers to the ZZZS, the employer also receives the decision of the appointed doctor. If the employee appeals against the decision of the ZZZS not to extend the sick leave and corresponding payments, there are significant delays in issuing new decisions. In that case, neither the worker nor the employer know whether the worker should come to work or whether sick leave continues. The situation is often resolved by using annual leave during the appeals process.

When a worker is on sick leave and his compensation is borne by the ZZZS, the employer has no obligations to him, he only has to pay him a holiday pay. Therefore, employers often instruct a worker to return to work only when they are completely healthy. During this time, they usually delegate work to other workers or hire new workers, and these procedures are usually complicated and time-consuming. Workers are therefore also hesitant to return to work, knowing that they will have to work at 100% capacity immediately. An employer cannot obtain information from a GP during sick leave, and the involvement of physicians and occupational medicine specialists is not common. Employers monitor the level of sick leave through lost working hours, keep their own records and can monitor trends by months and years.

The employer can also obtain detailed information on sick leaves for his company from the National Institute of Public Health. They also prepare an analysis of the sick leave by groups of diagnoses (Chapter ICD X.) It is also possible to compare the amount of sick leave to economic activity in Slovenia, by sex and age groups. This information is chargeable to the employer. The employer can use such information to plan workplace health promotion and occupational safety and health measures.

*The role of employers during disability assessment and in the vocational rehabilitation process*

When an employee has permanent health impairments, the GP presents him to the ZPIZ disability board. In this application procedure, the ZPIZ invites the employer to fill in a special form called work documentation (DD1). It contains a very detailed description of the work process and the objects of work, and also assesses the burdens and harms in the workplace, especially those that could affect the health of the worker. This document invites the employer to propose the transfer of the employee to another suitable position, to exercise the right to vocational rehabilitation and to make other comments and suggestions that are important for consideration by the Disability Commission. Employers often put down, in this document, that they do not have a suitable position for an employee with health problems and suggest disability retirement. Occupational safety professionals and occupational medicine practitioners typically fill in the part that relates to possible health impairments and requirements for the job. In 2019, 575 insured persons and 226 employers responded to the ZPIZ's invitation to the presentation of vocational rehabilitation. Among them, 332 insured persons expressed their interest in using the right to vocational rehabilitation and most of their employers supported them.

A ZPIZ expert prepares a preliminary opinion after reviewing the medical and work documentation. If vocational rehabilitation is a reasonable option for the employee (proposed by the employer, the GP, the insured person or the ZPIZ expert himself), as a right under the Act of ZPIZ, the ZPIZ invites the employer and the employee to a presentation of vocational rehabilitation options and procedures. At this occasion, the worker decides on his/her interest to participate in this process.

In the next step, the ZPIZ expert refers the employee to a vocational rehabilitation provider, who prepares a final report, which must clearly define the position on vocational rehabilitation, the method of implementation, the content and objectives, and the employer's opinion on the proposed vocational rehabilitation. In this procedure, the contractor preparing the professional report must contact the employer, present the possibilities and purpose of vocational rehabilitation and report on subsequent decisions with the signed consent of the employer. The employer then signs a tripartite contract with his employee and ZPIZ on vocational rehabilitation.

During the vocational rehabilitation process, the employee receives salary compensation from the ZPIZ. The rehabilitee is entitled to compensation for the duration of the process, which in 2019 averaged at EUR 590. The length of the process depends on the form of vocational rehabilitation, the longest option being formal education that can last up to two years. The employer can state that, after completing vocational rehabilitation, he will not have a suitable job for the worker. After completion of the process, he may terminate the employment contract with the prior consent of the Commission of determination of the grounds for termination of the employment contract. The employer has no obligations during this time.

The employer is involved in the part of vocational rehabilitation connected to the work process, as he has the best understanding of the possibilities how to implement the necessary improvements in the workplace. This is particularly evident in the provision of adjustments of the workplace with technical aids for the performance of the same profession or work, in practical work in the relevant workplace, and for in-service training in the relevant workplace. The employer's participation is also crucial in adjusting the work place or work resources needed to carry out vocational rehabilitation. When an employee receives training while working at a specific work place, the employer must offer another suitable job and present it to the senate of the disability commission with the form called work documentation (DD1).

### *Termination of a contract*

It is possible to dismiss employees during sick leave, but it does not happen very often due to very complicated regulations. According to the Employment Relationships Act, for an employee whose employment contract has been terminated due to business reasons or incapacity and who is absent from work due to illness or injury, the employment relationship shall end on the day the employee returns to work, or should return to work, but no later than six months after the expiry of the notice period. The termination is therefore for either business reasons or incapacity.

When workers enter disability insurance and return to work, employers may terminate their employment contract if they are unable to provide employees with a suitable job in accordance with the restrictions imposed by the Disability Commission. An employer who has five or fewer employees can do this on their own. In the case of larger employers, the Commission must give an opinion on the possible termination of employment in order to determine the grounds for termination of the employment contract. During the course of vocational rehabilitation, when disability insurance covers the remuneration for the employee, the employer may not terminate the employee's employment contract.

In almost three in four cases, the Disability Commission accepts the grounds for the termination of the employment contract (Table 5.10). The large majority or more than 90% of those laid off had a Category III disability status by ZPIZ classification. Most of those people should qualify for vocational rehabilitation. Proposals of ZPIZ Board of Examiners with significant restrictions, such as a ban on lifting heavy weights or no work in forced spinal postures, however, are often difficult for employers to meet.

Table 5.10. In three in four cases, the Disability Commission accepts the grounds for dismissal

Number of proposals for determining the grounds for termination of the employment contract and resolutions by the Disability Commission

| Year | Applications received in the current year | Positively resolved | Share | Negatively resolved | Share | Other outcome | Share | Total cases resolved |
|---|---|---|---|---|---|---|---|---|
| 2006 | 1 133 | 599 | 73% | 160 | 19% | 64 | 8% | 823 |
| 2007 | 839 | 723 | 77% | 166 | 18% | 49 | 5% | 938 |
| 2008 | 866 | 572 | 73% | 142 | 18% | 70 | 9% | 784 |
| 2009 | 1 156 | 913 | 80% | 150 | 13% | 78 | 7% | 1 141 |
| 2010 | 964 | 717 | 73% | 178 | 18% | 88 | 9% | 983 |
| 2011 | 712 | 589 | 72% | 176 | 21% | 54 | 7% | 819 |
| 2012 | 698 | 479 | 71% | 141 | 21% | 55 | 8% | 675 |
| 2013 | 658 | 495 | 71% | 140 | 20% | 59 | 9% | 694 |
| 2014 | 621 | 440 | 68% | 180 | 28% | 30 | 5% | 650 |
| 2015 | 441 | 282 | 62% | 147 | 33% | 23 | 5% | 452 |
| 2016 | 445 | 293 | 64% | 129 | 28% | 33 | 7% | 455 |
| 2017 | 458 | 303 | 66% | 119 | 26% | 35 | 8% | 457 |
| 2018 | 301 | 268 | 68% | 101 | 26% | 23 | 6% | 392 |
| 2019 | 451 | 301 | 72% | 98 | 23% | 20 | 5% | 419 |
| Total | 9 743 | 6 974 | 72% | 2 027 | 21% | 681 | 7% | 9 682 |

Note: A positively resolved case means that the employer cannot offer a new employment contract for business reasons so there is a basis for termination of the employment contract. Negatively resolved case is the opposite, so there is no justifiable reason to terminate the contract. The most common of other outcomes is the withdrawal of the claim by the employer.
Source: OECD calculations based on University Rehabilitation Institute Republic of Slovenia (URI-Soča) data www.ir-rs.si/.

StatLink https://stat.link/0vrmij

### 5.5.2. Occupational physicians are underutilised in Slovenia

*Legal developments and requirements*

Occupational, traffic and sports medicine has a long tradition in Slovenia, dating back to the 18th century and the mercury mines of Idrija. In 1971, the Institute of Occupational Medicine was established. During this time, occupational medicine was part of the public health system. In the course of the social transition in 1991 and the Health Care and Health Insurance Act of the time, occupational medicine was annulled and reversible clinics were abolished. Occupational medicine was considered a remnant of the socialist system and corresponding activities transferred to the free market. Doctors specialising in occupational medicine concluded contracts with employers to perform their activity. Such an arrangement has remained to this day.

The Occupational Safety and Health Act of 1999 reintroduced occupational medicine activities into Slovenian legislation. With this law, last amended in 2011, the responsibility for occupational medicine came from the Ministry of Health to the Ministry of Labour, Family and Social Affairs. Today, there are approximately 190 occupational medicine specialists in Slovenia, most of them working directly with employers (only some work in the public health network). The director of the public institution in which these occupational doctors work conclude the contracts with employers.

An occupational physician is a health care provider in the field of occupational, transport and sports medicine entrusted by the employer to implement measures related to health at work. The tasks performed of an occupational doctor depends on the type of activity performed by the employer and the type and level of risk of accidents at work, occupational and work-related diseases. The majority of occupational physicians, while engaged in drafting the expert basis for the safety statement, are however mostly performing health examinations or health check-ups of workers. Employers shall provide workers with health examinations corresponding to their occupational health and safety risks.

There is quite a bit of ambiguity in this area, as occupational doctors also determine the general health condition of employees. The law also requires the occupational doctor to determine the special health requirements that a worker must meet in an individual workplace (without any clear guidance on the definition of special health requirements). In agreement with the Ministry of Labour, Family, Social Affair and Equal Opportunities, the Ministry of Health adopted an executive act, the Rules on Preventive Medical Examinations of Workers, which defines the types, scope and content of preventive medical examinations of workers and the manner and deadlines for performing these inspections. In practice, the employer determines the scope of preventive examinations on the proposal of an occupational doctor, in accordance with the risk assessment.

### Everyday work in practice

Occupational physicians should inform workers on the risks related to the working environment, and the extent to which the work could lead to functional impairment, diseases or disability. In Slovenia, on the contrary, occupational physicians are not included in monitoring and analysing the situation related to occupational and work-related diseases – which fall under the remit of GPs. Sometimes occupational doctors draft reports for employers on findings resulting from analysis of the workers' health status determined during health examinations. Such reports can contain proposals for the improvement of the work process aimed at complementing or upgrading the measures related to health at work.

Occupational physicians should also participate in the disability assessment, vocational rehabilitation process and advice on the selection of other appropriate work, but this is not usually the case. They are engaged in the preparation of the employer's plan for first aid provision and participate in worker and employer training on general and specific first aid measures. In the execution of tasks, occupational doctors should co-operate with the worker's GP and with disability and health insurance expert bodies, exchanging data on workers' health status and helping to determine the justification of temporary or permanent absence from work and to assess the ability to work. Based on the worker's prior written consent, the occupational doctor may obtain access to information on the worker's health, treatment and rehabilitation from the worker's GP. In turn, the occupational doctor shall communicate to the worker's GP, on request, information on the worker's workload and workplace requirements (which is necessary for the sickness and disability procedures).

### Involvement in the return-to-work process

During sick leave, occupational physicians are not included in programmes or procedures to promote the worker's return to work. In the sick-leave process, all services (treatment, rehabilitation, benefits) are under the responsibility of ZZZS. Occupational physicians are not part of the health insurance system, which thus cannot reimburse any of their services. Not involving occupational physicians in the return-to-work process is a missed opportunity but the consequence of the legislative changes in 1991, described above.

Occupational physicians, working in the field of worker health protection, are not included in the process of disability assessment and vocational rehabilitation in a systematic way. Their exclusion from the disability process is another missed opportunity. The only exception are occupational physicians who work in teams of vocational rehabilitation providers and in the Institute for Rehabilitation of the Republic of Slovenia (URI-Soča), Center for Vocational rehabilitation (CPR), unit Ljubljana and Maribor.

## References

Card, D., J. Kluve and A. Weber (2010), "Active Labour Market Policy Evaluations: A Meta-Analysis", *The Economic Journal*, Vol. 120/548, pp. F452-F477, http://dx.doi.org/10.1111/j.1468-0297.2010.02387.x. [3]

Južnik Rotar, L. (2011), "Effectiveness of the Public Work Program in Slovenia", *Managing Global Transitions*, Vol. 9/3. [2]

MDDSZ (2016), *Bela knjiga o pokojninah (White Paper on Pension System Development)*, Lubjana, April, http://www.mddsz.gov.si/nc/si/medijsko_sredisce/novica/article/1939/7901/. [1]

## Notes

[1] It is important to point out ambiguities in the terminology of vocational rehabilitation in Slovenia. The term vocational rehabilitation is officially only used for procedures regulated by the Pension and Disability Act, as it is precisely defined only in that act. In Slovenia, the term employment rehabilitation is used for the field of employment of persons according to the Vocational Rehabilitation and Employment of Persons with Disability Act. Internationally, the comparable term would also be vocational rehabilitation. There is no single term for the return-to-work processes that take place within the framework of medical rehabilitation at URI-Soča, although the experts use the term vocational rehabilitation.

[2] The Standards for Vocational Rehabilitation Services define professional principles, the vocational rehabilitation process, its content, work methods and techniques, the expected results, as well as the fundamental professional and organisational conditions of service provision.

[3] Such companies must have at least 40% of their workforce classified as a person with disability. Employment centres offer special form of employment under special conditions (sheltered employment).

[4] Vocational rehabilitation has been part of rehabilitation activities in URI-Soča since its establishment in 1954. After the year 1984, it has been reorganised as an independent section in two regional units, in Ljubljana and Maribor.